MW01490161

FROSTY
My Spirit Guide

FROSTY
My Spirit Guide

How Changing Our Perceptions of Death
Can Bring Us More Love, Joy, Happiness and Life!

BETHANY-ELIZABETH FAYE HANSEN

BALBOA.
PRESS
A DIVISION OF HAY HOUSE

Copyright © 2011 Bethany-Elizabeth Faye Hansen

All rights reserved. No part of this book may be used or reproduced by
any means, graphic, electronic, or mechanical, including photocopying,
recording, taping or by any information storage retrieval system
without the written permission of the publisher except in the case
of brief quotations embodied in critical articles and reviews.

Balboa Press books may be ordered through booksellers or by contacting:

Balboa Press
A Division of Hay House
1663 Liberty Drive
Bloomington, IN 47403
www.balboapress.com
1-(877) 407-4847

Because of the dynamic nature of the Internet, any web addresses or
links contained in this book may have changed since publication and
may no longer be valid. The views expressed in this work are solely those
of the author and do not necessarily reflect the views of the publisher,
and the publisher hereby disclaims any responsibility for them.

The author of this book does not dispense medical advice or prescribe the use
of any technique as a form of treatment for physical, emotional, or medical
problems without the advice of a physician, either directly or indirectly. The
intent of the author is only to offer information of a general nature to help
you in your quest for emotional and spiritual well-being. In the event you use
any of the information in this book for yourself, which is your constitutional
right, the author and the publisher assume no responsibility for your actions.

Any people depicted in stock imagery provided by Thinkstock are models,
and such images are being used for illustrative purposes only.
Certain stock imagery © Thinkstock.

ISBN: 978-1-4525-4050-4 (e)
ISBN: 978-1-4525-3959-1 (sc)
ISBN: 978-1-4525-3960-7 (hc)

Library of Congress Control Number: 2011918127

Printed in the United States of America

Balboa Press rev. date: 11/17/2011

For Frosty...

(Aka Frizzy)

and

Faye, Glenn, Jami,
Shaun and Emily,
and all our loved ones in spirit
who work daily to let us know...

"I'm still here."

FOREWORD

Where does the word *death* come from anyway? Why do we call it death and what makes people dead? They are more alive than we are. We've all heard the expression, "It was like hugging a dead tree." Well, some people who are living are dead—or seem like they are.

Why are we so afraid of death? Is it the word *death*—the way it feels on our tongue or the way the word death *feels* to us? Why are we not able to celebrate our loved ones' transition into a higher level of being? Is it only because we think we are being separated from them—that they are being ripped away from us? But just because we think they are—does that mean that they actually are?

Joy is for the living, and transitioning into spirit is euphoric with joy. This book is about connecting with those that we love. It's about realizing that we are still connected and always can be. It's about believing in our loved ones' love for us, and that they have transitioned to help us and to teach us about being more in our hearts. All we have to do is stop—just stop, and listen, using our hearts instead of our minds.

Just stop, then listen....

Can you hear them...?

∾ CHAPTER 1 ∾

*I*t was 12:43 p.m. when the vet called. I had been antsy all morning, just wanting to get Frizz home. Part of me was screaming, *"Hurry, hurry faster; get there in time."* The other part said no way it could ever—would never—happen. God wouldn't do that. *God just wouldn't do that,* the little voice inside my head kept screaming. *What kind of a God would take him now?* But the call did come. I grabbed shoes, socks, and my car keys and drove as fast as I dared. The vet's office was only four minutes away, but the drive seemed endless. I was still divided. The intuitive part of me knew he would already be gone by the time I got there; the human part was screaming to hold on, just hold on a few minutes longer. *Please, please, please, just let me get there in time.*

∾ CHAPTER 2 ∾

*I*t was too late. I knew it the minute I walked in. I knew it in the way everyone was looking not at me, but down at the floor. I didn't want to believe it. I just couldn't accept it. My mind refused to go there. I knew shock was setting in to protect me. This was too much to deal with. Frosty and I had been constant companions for sixteen years. Where I went, he went; where he went, I went. Love was our constant connection. He was my soul mate, my spirit guide, my friend, and my partner. We were the perfect set of twins. I knelt down next to the cage. I didn't know what to do or say.

The vet, the technicians, and the assistants were all standing around, watching and waiting to witness my grief. *Leave! Get out!* My mind screamed at them. Just leave. They didn't understand how close Frosty and I were. They didn't understand that this was a private thing between Frosty and me. I mustered up the courage to turn to the vet and say, "I want to be alone with him." The vet hesitated, but they all slowly got up and left.

I sat on the floor, wanting to climb into the cage to hold my dearest friend and feel the last remains of life in his body, but I couldn't fit beside him in the cage. I had to get him out of there, have him to myself, and be alone with him, just me and him. Maybe I could reach him. Maybe I could bring him back and give us just one more day.

Why wasn't I feeling him? I had been a practicing psychic medium for a long time; it had always seemed so easy to talk with other souls who had transitioned into spirit. Why wasn't this happening with Frizz and me now? Never mind it'd only been five minutes, I just wanted to hear him and know he was okay.

The vet came back in and chatted with me about Frosty, his condition, and what had happened. I didn't want to talk, and I didn't want to talk to him. I couldn't stand to pretend; I was too numb. My mouth wasn't working, and I didn't want it to. I felt anger toward him. The whys were already setting in. Why hadn't he called me sooner? Why had he let Frizzy die, and why had he pushed so hard to keep him there the last few days? I was still sitting there, numb on the floor of the vet's office with my best friend, and already the anger and the blame were rearing their ugly heads. How had it come to this?

I never thought this day would come, yet of course I knew it would some day. The little signs had started months before. The bigger signs, which were subtle and quiet, had started almost a year ago to the day. Frosty had begun having trouble riding in the van. He had always done so well in the past, but now he would pant, when the van was moving. I kept telling myself it was motion sickness or not enough air flowing through the van. I kept the tires inflated for the smoothest ride, the air conditioner on high, and the windows down. These things seemed to stabilize him for a while, so we continued to travel, but staying closer to home.

In March, he started having more allergy and cold issues. Antibiotics helped and kept him doing pretty well, but on the vet's recommendation, I decided to run allergy tests on him. The results showed that he was allergic to many things in his food and environment. I changed his food, switched the bedding to protect against dust mites, and began running an allergen remover in the bedroom.

It was easy to tell myself this was going to resolve everything, and he was going to be much better: back to perfect health. Frosty would feel great, and we would get back to normal. It was easy because that was the only thing I wanted to hear.

Frosty knew what was really going on, and while I was making changes in the bedroom, he lay there, watching me, telling me with his wise eyes, *Things are changing. Can you hear me? Things are changing.*

I had always listened to and been able to hear Frosty. I talked to him just like I would a person. To me animals are aware and can and do communicate just fine—great, in fact! The hours of quiet meditation they put in every day, just being still, just waiting to receive wisdom from their creator and hopefully be able to pass it on to us, gives them a miraculous ability to communicate.

Well, this time I wasn't having any part in listening to what Frosty was telling me. My mind was just not capable of going to a place that would be a place without him. It had always been "where I go, Frizzy goes." I was sticking to that, and that's all there was to it.

So we continued on as usual. Frosty was better after the allergy testing, so when the opportunity arose to be present for a granddaughter's birth, in Utah, we hit the road. The trip started off okay, but about three hours into the drive, I started thinking it might be too much. It was a nine-hour drive, so we just took our time, and once there, I hoped he would be able to relax and be okay with the trip back. We were only in Utah a day when I received an emergency call from home. The rest I had hoped for was not coming. Going back so quickly, without any rest in between, was too much for Frosty, and it was an extremely rough trip back. I realized then I never should have taken him so far from home, and that this was to be the last long-distance trip that we take.

When we got home, Frosty was exhausted. It took a few weeks for him to recover, but even in recovering, he was never quite the same. His breathing in the car became mostly panting; normal breathing was a strain. Our trips to the park became strolls in the neighborhood as his legs ached (or so I wanted to believe) and he was slowing way down. I could tell he was in pain a lot of the time. The vet couldn't find anything wrong, and all blood tests showed nothing, so it was chalked up to Frosty getting older. My heart knew there was something wrong, but I continued to focus on and pray for his health.

Another big change after our trip to Utah was that Frosty began sleeping part of the night on the floor. He would get off and on the bed, or stay there part of the night and then get down. Clearly something had changed. We had slept on the same bed since he was about four weeks old. It was painful for me, I didn't understand what was going on or why things had changed. Being human I took it personally, popping back and forth from feeling hurt, anger and concern. I tried everything I could to change it—including sleeping with chicken in my hand. Yes, I really did. It was amazing what lengths I was willing to go to, to hold onto what was normal. Frosty, being the one with all the wisdom, learned that he could sleep on the floor all night and then jump up on the bed in the morning to con me with his barks and yelps, his way of communicating and conning me, easily of course into giving him the chicken.

My heart knew Frosty sleeping on the floor had nothing to do with me. My heart knew he wasn't mad at me. I knew he was separating, but again, I was not going to let my mind go there. I'm sure, in God's wisdom, separating somewhat at that point would make the physical separation easier when the time came. Frosty pulling back on sleeping with me was one of the bigger signs that showed me things were going to change.

It was the beginning of June when I received another message, or sign, that time was important. My girlfriend sent me an e-mail about Christian the lion. It was appearing on the Internet, but since I don't use the Internet much, I hadn't heard about it. It was about a lion named Christian that was raised by two people in their home until he got too big. Then they were forced to release him into the wild. Time went by, and they decided to go back to see the lion. Before they got there, they were told that, because of the mental makeup of a lion and the fact that Christian by then had a pride of his own, he would not remember them. Surprising them all, and once again showing that love has no limits, Christian did remember them. I cried as I watched the video, knowing this was another message that Frosty's transition time was coming, but that he would know me and I him after his transition. My heart got the message, but once again, my mind shut down the divine guidance that was coming into my soul. I was afraid. I was coming from fear. It was fear that came from a perceived sense of separation and loss.

I deleted the e-mail, pushing it to the back of my mind, while placing it in my heart, remembering it, but refusing to go there. I just wasn't ready. It just added to the panic I was already feeling and made the screaming in my head a little louder.

Later that month was when the next big sign came to me, this one even bigger than the last, rocking me to my core and feeding the panic that was already growing inside me. I had already become more protective about my time, wanting only to spend time with Frizz. Going anywhere even for a short time, while Frosty waited in the van, was hard on both of us. When I got to the designated location for my appointment that evening, I went about setting Frosty up as usual, giving him water, toys, and things that he needed before I left the van. I was feeling especially uptight that night about leaving him. I wanted to cancel, but it had to do with some work I had been doing and I felt I had to be there. I was friendly with the people I was meeting, but that really didn't make it any easier.

There was an air conditioner in the van that ran off a generator to keep Frosty cool in the summertime. A friend had come up with the idea of putting a cell phone in with the generator. The phone was set up on auto answer, so I could call it and the phone would answer itself. I could hear the generator running and know Frosty's air conditioner was keeping him cool.

On this night when I got out of the van, I knelt down to put Frosty's phone inside the generator case. I had my own personal phone in my hand, so I put it down, to set up the other phone. I shut the door to the generator, and then picked up my phone. It felt funny in my hand when I picked it up, like it was empty. I looked at it and the picture of Frosty that was always on the front was gone. The panic went through me so hard that it was difficult to stand up. That was the moment when I knew, and for an instant, my mind let it in. The voice inside my head was screaming so loudly that I couldn't think. The panic was unreal.

I scrolled through the phone, looking for the picture that had been on the front so I could put it back. I kept telling myself, *If I can just get it back, then everything will be okay.* The picture was gone not only from the front of my phone but also from the media section on my phone. Throughout the evening, I kept trying to get it back. It was hard to concentrate on anything.

It was business with friends, but it was still business. I forced myself to stay, yet I was antsy about getting back to the van.

One of the friends who was there agreed to come back to the house to help me with the picture. Finally after a few hours, calls to Verizon, and my friend figuring it all out, the picture of Frosty was back on the phone; neither my friend nor the people at Verizon could figure out what had happened. *Divine messaging,* I called it.

Once the picture was back on, I felt calmer, but something inside had kicked me in the gut, a little shred of my inner peace was gone, and my unconscious awareness had shifted and opened up just a little bit more, bringing my fears closer to the surface in my head.

Looking back, I can see how that evening would have been a good time to stop, get quiet, and listen. Frosty knew his time for transitioning into spirit was coming and if I had asked him or asked in prayer, the answer probably would have come.

Awareness and courage are two important keys to acceptance. If I had awareness and courage then, would I have accepted? I don't know, probably not. I'm still human.

After that night, just five months from Frosty's transition date, I started eating more, watching more television, and staying in more. I didn't want to leave him, yet I was afraid to be with him, afraid of what I would see. It was like I was freezing up, unable to move yet running at the same time. I never said it out loud, but my mind repeated it a hundred times a day. I just wanted to be alone with Frizzy. I didn't want to share him or my time with anyone. I wanted to spend every minute with him.

I started sleeping on the floor so I could be near him. He still kept some distance, but I felt closer to him physically on the floor. I slept on the floor as long as my back would allow, eventually shifting back and forth from the floor to the bed. Frosty knew I was struggling, so on the nights my back wouldn't allow me to be on the floor, he would sleep next to the bed and I would sleep at the foot of the bed, allowing me to sleep with my hand on his back. It was a way I could feel more connected to him.

When friends asked me to go places or to do things with them I said, no. I wanted to spend time with Frosty. The thought that kept coming was that I would spend time with friends after Frosty was gone. I never stopped to think about why I thought that. All I knew was the thought kept popping up. I didn't want to look at or ask myself why, not then. I knew everyone would transition into spirit at one time or another. Of course the time for Frosty's transition was a ways off, or so I told myself. I desperately wanted to believe it; I clung to that thought, which made it harder for him, but, in my human mind, that was the best I could do at the time.

The thoughts in my head were coming in more quickly, but my gut was kicking me harder to listen. The fear was so great that I kept my gut silenced by giving it fast food and sugar. I silenced the yelling in my head by turning up the television. I didn't realize at the time, that I was also blocking out my connection with Frizz, giving up time with him and yes, I do have guilt about that. I was working as a psychic, I should have known, I should have acknowledged, but I was too afraid.

A few months before things came to a head, Frosty developed a sore on the back of his right rear foot. The doctor thought it was an allergy or an infection of some kind at first, so Frosty was given more antibiotics. It took that round of antibiotics before we realized arthritis was causing him to walk differently.

I don't know the reason the thing with his foot made the thought come that our time together was limited, but it did. I was again too scared to ask myself what that meant— because of the sore, our time was limited? But I knew, as we all do, but fear was clouding my ability to see what was really going on. I put a doggie sock on Frizz, which he adjusted to quickly and was perfectly happy with. It gave us the freedom of taking our walks on the beach, at the park, or in the neighborhood without any worry of his foot getting infected. Frosty loved being outdoors; he knew what was good for him. The sun, the trees, the water, and I were his days.

∽ CHAPTER 3 ∽

*I*n September we took our last overnight trip to San Diego. I didn't know at the time that it was our last trip—I wasn't allowing it into my head—but my heart knew because that little voice kept telling me. We had been staying at the same hotel, The Kona Kai Resort on Shelter Island, for the past five years. The operations manager Dennis had been reserving the same two rooms for us. The rooms were set up in a way that made it easy for me to take Frosty, and any family or friends who came along on our weekends away from home. For Frosty and me, those trips were just years of gifts and happy times. In San Diego, we would hang out on the beach and just basically love life. There were seagulls for Frizz to play with and moments of quiet connection and meditation that brought us both closer to God. It was always fun, sun, and fresh air, and we looked forward to going once a month or so. Frosty knew the routine and looked forward to keeping me on that same routine. If I differed from it at all, he would let me know. Once when I tried to carry the bags in, before taking him into the room, he climbed up into the front seat and barked and barked and barked. He was telling me I had forgotten something—like I would ever forget him. Another time I had left his friend, his favorite stuffed bunny, in the van. He stood at the door, staring out at the van, telling me his bunny was in one place and he was in another. He knew the routine and he insisted on sticking to it.

This weekend was a little different in that I had not invited any friends to come with us or made any plans to meet with any. I was feeling very emotional about the weekend. I didn't want to share Frizz with anyone. It was like I was savoring every second, memorizing everything about being there with my sweet, precious Frizzy. I took the camcorder in and shot lots of video; we did our walks as usual, maybe a little more than usual; and when he woke me up at 3:00 a.m. for a walk, I focused on gratitude instead of how cold it was outside. There were many gifts about that trip, but one of the greatest is that the room had a king-size bed so Frosty still slept on the bed. It was big enough to give him that sense of still doing his job of trying to separate, yet made it okay for him to stay on the bed at night. That meant in the morning we would play our wake-up game of me blowing in his face and him barking his commands at me. We played tug-of-war and he barked at the seagulls. We would laugh and all seemed perfect in the world. He always slept more at the beach. It was like he would go into a deep meditation and be rejuvenated when he woke up. I planted every minute in my head, cemented it there for future use. I sat with him a lot and I looked at him a lot. At the end of our three days, as usual, neither one of us wanted to leave, but this time was harder; I kept putting off going.

Our normal routine when we left The Kona Kai was for me to load up the van and then take Frosty out. We would go for a walk and then I would get him in the van and make a quick trip back to the room to check that we had everything, to express gratitude and love for the beautiful room, and lock up and leave. This time we went for a walk, and then I loaded up the van. I wanted Frosty with me when we left and, as I knelt down in prayer next to my precious Frosty, the sobs came, making it hard to pray. I probably knew but was still hanging on to the hope that we would be able to go back again, sometime soon. Our prayer of gratitude went on longer than usual. I had to pray for the will to get up and leave. It took a while before I could stand up, but when I did,

I felt a wave of strength come over me. I grabbed Frosty's leash and with tears in my eyes we walked out together.

It had been a couple of weeks since our overnight trip to San Diego when I felt the urgency to go back to San Diego, just for a day trip. It was a Friday when this thought came to me, and the next morning I loaded up and we headed down.

We stopped halfway down just to make it easier on Frosty. I could see he wasn't feeling that good. It was starting to show more and more that something was wrong. His strength always amazed me, even when he wasn't feeling good—he was still always so happy when we would go in the van. He loved to go places!

He was better once we got to San Diego and he could get out of the van. It was a nice day, so I pulled out a blanket and we sat next to the beach in the sun, right across from our room at The Kona Kai hotel on Shelter Island. Frosty slept a lot, but it gave me quiet time with him and a chance to just breathe him in and look at him. I kept hugging him and touching him and doing the mushy thing with him, which is a game we always played. It was a very peaceful day filled with strength and acceptance. I saw a quiet peace in Frosty when we left, and I knew he knew way more than I wanted to know.

Normally for our day trips we would hang out across from our room, and today was no exception. In the past Frosty would tug at the leash and try to drag me to our room. But on this day, he seemed content to lie in the sun and, even as we left, he didn't tug to go to our room. Looking back, that was another sign that he knew something that I wasn't yet ready to accept.

I will always be grateful for that day because, when I think of it, it brings me peace, connection, strength, and insight to the wisdom that our furry friends truly do have.

∾ CHAPTER 4 ∾

A few days after our day trip to San Diego, Frosty had another recheck with the vet for his allergies. Afterward, with the news that he was doing well, we headed to Dana Point to meet a friend for a walk. Frosty loved Dana Point, which was our substitute for San Diego. He loved our friend Melissa, who we were meeting that night—he knew he would get cookies from her. So with relief after the vet visit and the excitement to go, we were off for a nighttime walk.

It was dark when we got there, but that didn't seem to bother Frosty. Melissa and I were amazed at how strong he seemed and how far he walked, tugging on the leash the whole time. It was me who finally said, "Let's take him back." Frosty wanted to keep walking, but I was concerned because he had been acting like he wasn't feeling well. I had to tug him pretty hard to get him to turn around to go back to the van.

BETHANY-ELIZABETH FAYE HANSEN

I was uneasy, feeling worried because he was acting as if this was his last time to be in Dana Point. I'm sure in his wise, all-knowing wisdom, Frosty did know that this was the last time that he would be there in his earthly form.

It's amazing to look back and see that it was less than a week later that our world would change so fast. I've heard it said that things can change in the blink of an eye ….

Well, it's true.

∾ CHAPTER 5 ∾

*I*t was a Tuesday, just two days before everything permanently changed for us. We spent most of the day out front working on our little garden, planting flowers, and cleaning the waterfall. Frosty had been doing really well and he was going back and forth from the inside to the outside. He would come out, nose around for snacks, and hang out right in front of me, talking to me while I planted, which he did a lot when we were outside. He loved being outside and he loved the flowers. Out in the yard that day, he sniffed each one that was planted and gave his seal of approval. When he wasn't out front, he would stand in the front doorway, saying, "Come on, Mama, come inside. When he tired of doing that, he would lie in the front window, watching for a while before he would come back out again. He preferred lying in the front window, resting his chin on the windowsill, to lying on the sidewalk.

It was while he was stealing snacks from his snack buddy that I snapped a picture that was a sign of something still to come. I took the picture from my phone and sent it off to a friend. It was later that night that she called me, amazed by the picture. The way the picture had been taken, it looked to her as if there was an angel in the background. She had me pull it up again to look at it and indeed, it did look as if there was an angel standing behind Frosty in the picture. It looked angelic and it screamed something at me. For a split second I heard my heart say, *Frosty's going to transition soon.* I heard it in a way that was so clear, but no way; my mind blocked it out. When another friend saw it and commented on Frosty's guardian angel being so close, she was kidding, but it was chipping away at me. Each time I pulled up the picture, the angel screamed at me to pay attention, to listen, but my refusal to go there was solidly in place and my fear was just too great to hear my own heart.

I kept telling myself Frosty was going to be around at least another year or two. His dad Bam Bam lived in body until he was almost twenty, and Frosty was going to, as well, so we had plenty of time.

❦ CHAPTER 6 ❦

The morning of October 21 was the day everything changed. We got up, as usual, Frosty ate, and we went out in the yard for him to do his business and sniff around just a bit. He actually seemed better. When he came in, we played tug-of-war and the barking game. I felt hopeful and it seemed like he did too. Since it seemed like he was feeling better, I decided to take a few minutes to dig out some pictures that I'd been wanting to get out of the office closet. Frosty would go into the office once in awhile, but he loved the bedroom with the big window where he could see outside. The window was low to the ground, and with the windows open it was like being outside, so he stayed there most of the time, which is why I kept putting off digging through the office closet. Today he did his normal thing when I was in the office, which was to play peek-a-boo and try to get me to give up going in there. To get him to come with me, I would kneel outside the bedroom door and bark at him until he would chase after me. When I got to the office door, I would flip around and blow in his face, which would make him bark right up in mine. Up to that point, that morning was no different than any other morning. In fact, like I said, all seemed better than it had been in a while.

It was after finding the pictures and coming back into the bedroom that I saw something was wrong. He was standing up by the window, but he had a funny look on his face and he was standing differently on his back legs, like he was pulling them in toward his stomach. I looked at him, trying to get my brain to work, but it seemed to be freezing up. I said, "What's wrong, Frizz?" It was like he couldn't talk to me. He was frozen too. He crossed the bedroom going slowly back and forth, and as I watched him, it was like the back end of him was freezing up, making it hard for him to walk. It started with his back legs shaking and then finally giving way. If you have ever watched someone you love collapse, you know how it feels. Frosty crossed the bedroom one more time and I saw the weak, shaky feeling take over his whole body, and he collapsed to the floor. I dropped what I had in my hands and grabbed for him and the phone all in one motion. I pulled him on my lap so I could calm him. The thought rolled through my head that this was it. He was going to die right here and now, lying in my lap. I looked into his eyes and they were moving back and forth so fast that I was sure, this really was it. But as I looked at him, he still seemed to be in there and he was amazingly calm. I tried to mirror that. I held him while talking to him and fighting off the urge to check out myself. A few times I had thought that when Frosty's time came, it would be peaceful and in his sleep, with me there with him. This wasn't quite the way I had pictured it.

I called the vet to see if he could come to me because I knew I could not get Frosty in the car on my own. The vet was out of the office, so I had to get Frosty there. I called my oldest son, praying he would answer his phone. I knew I was going to need help getting Frosty into the van, as by this point he could not stand at all. My son didn't answer. I tried my girlfriend who lived just a few doors down, all the while holding Frosty and praying that this wasn't it. My girlfriend didn't answer, so I tried my son again—still no answer. I tried my girlfriend one more time. She answered and came right down. I called the vet again, realizing between the two of us we still could not lift Frosty on our own. I kept screaming in my head for my son to come home, for God to send him home. I knew he could lift Frosty into the van on his own, and he has a calm, angelic, connection with animals that I knew Frosty would respond to. I called the vet again and they suggested my girlfriend come pick up one of the techs to bring back to the house to help lift Frosty into the van.

She left and I sat with Frizz, praying for him and for my son to come home. I was holding him on my lap, which isn't easy, as he weighed about seventy pounds, but I wanted to hold onto him. I was concerned he might try to stand up. I admit I was scared and it didn't occur to me to ask what was happening inside Frosty's body. I just prayed and talked to him; he seemed so calm.

Miracles do happen, because just then the front door opened and in walked my son. I looked up at him and said, "Why are you home?" He said, "I got into an argument with my boss." I said, "Oh, would you put Frosty in the van for me?" He looked at Frosty and me sitting on the floor, which was not an unusual sight. My son was confused at first, and then he walked around to where he could see Frosty's face. He knelt down, looking at Frosty. I started to explain as he picked him up and headed out the front door toward the van. I was grateful as I was finding it hard to talk and was grateful that my son came home for whatever the reason.

The vet was less than five minutes away, but it seemed to take forever. When we pulled into the parking lot, the vet's assistant came right out with a gurney to get Frosty inside. My son, who had sat on the floor of the van with Frizz, got out, picked him up and carried him past the gurney and inside where the vet was waiting.

The vet had me remove his harness and chain and my son placed him on the X-ray table. They wanted to see if there was something going on inside his head. I was asked to leave the room while the X-ray was taken and blood was drawn. None of this medical stuff was new to me, but being separated from Frosty was. We had been separated only a couple of times and now wasn't the time to start. It was agony wondering if Frosty knew I was there, holding him in my mind and praying that he wasn't hurting and that he would be okay.

It seemed like forever, as those kinds of situations always do, before the vet finally came out, bringing the X-rays with him. He said there was only a small spot, but other than that were normal signs of aging. We would have to wait a day for the blood test results to come back. He believed it was an infection and he wanted to keep Frosty overnight, maybe even for a few days, to treat him with intravenous antibiotics. Overnight. Oh, God. This was not the time for me to leave him. The idea of not being there for him now was almost more than I could humanly stand or do, but I knew it had to be. I was sure Frosty was thinking I had left him and wasn't coming back. Of course that was the human side of me thinking from my panicky, fearful place.

I told the doctor I needed to see Frosty and he agreed, as long as I made it short. He said it was hard on the animals each time the owner left. Frosty wagged his tail when I came in. That was a good sign: he knew who I was. I kept telling him I was there for him, that I would be right outside, that all he had to do was close his eyes and he would see me. He seemed fairly calm, raising his head to look at me and wagging his tail off and on. His eyes had slowed down in the moving back and forth, but I wondered if he was dizzy.

The vet came in and told me they needed to get the IV started, and that it would be better if I wasn't there. I hugged Frizz tightly again and told him I would be right outside. The vet assured me that Frosty would be going home with me soon. I had to trust that, for at that moment I didn't know the end was near. I walked out carrying his harness, feeling like I was going to have a heart attack. I wondered how Frosty really was and what he was thinking, and I wished I could do more for him. I forced myself to take deep breaths and put my focus on my precious Frizzy, willing him to be better now. I wasn't sure when he would come home, but I put my attention and focus into being grateful that he was now home.

My son and my girlfriend were waiting in the vet's lobby for me. I couldn't talk. I didn't want to talk. We walked out in silence, with my mind screaming to Frosty that I was with him.

When I got to the house, I headed for the shower—water had a way of calming me down and I needed to calm down, breathe deeply, and collect my thoughts. I knew I was going to have to fight the panic I was feeling and that was threatening to take over.

A crazy thought kept screaming at me—at least I thought it was crazy, or wanted to believe it was crazy: *this is the beginning of the end.* My mind kept screaming, *No, no, no.* I had to stay positive; I was not going to let myself sink into that hole. I put on my positive-thinking CD, which is a part of *The Love Tape* series, and started saying affirmations in my head: *Frosty is healthy and strong and in complete health now.* I probably should have called friends for support, but I didn't want to. I didn't want to talk with anyone. I was too filled with fear that they might think negative thoughts, and I couldn't bear that right now.

I forced myself to move, to do some errands like getting Frosty food, new toys, and new rugs for the van. I found that being gone from the bedroom for more than an hour made me feel crazy, so I would go to one place, then go back and sit in the bedroom, praying and putting focus into seeing Frosty well and home. Then I would get back in the van and sit in the parking lot of the vet's office praying, writing affirmations, and writing Frosty and God letters. I wanted to be close to Frosty so I could talk to him in my mind and send him healing thoughts. Then I would force myself to go do more things to prepare for him to be home again.

Thursday was the easiest day, if there was such a thing as an easier day. I had seen and been with him until about one in the afternoon, but with nighttime and darkness came more panic that was even harder to fight off. I decided I better call someone who could help keep me focused on the positive. I called my girlfriend Shelley in Arizona and she held my hand for hours. Of course I still went back and forth between the calm and the panic, but being on the phone with her forced me to keep going back to the calm. She kept reminding to stay calm for Frosty's sake.

I stayed in the parking lot until one in the morning. I called upon God and all my spirit guides and Frosty's too. My girlfriend Faye had always been my biggest support, which was amazing because she had transitioned into spirit almost thirty years ago. She's been my main form of validation that our loved ones are still with us and that they are there for us when we need them. She is an animal lover and I am sure she had a hand in sending Frosty to me all those years ago. I talked with her a lot knowing, she was with Frosty and able to be in the cage with him. He was always comforted by her presence, and it was her being with him now that I clung to. To Frosty, having Faye with him was like having me with him.

It was around one o'clock when I finally forced myself to go home. It helped being in the bedroom where Frosty had always been, and yet it hurt at the same time. I was too worried to sleep, but I knew I had to at least lie down.

Friday morning was a little more nerve racking, as I was ready for him to come home. My mind was set on him coming home that day, but the vet had other ideas. I called in the morning and he said he wanted to keep Frosty another day, as there had been only a slight change. His eyes had stopped moving back and forth in his head, but he still was unable to stand and he wasn't eating. My nerves were getting the best of me. I hadn't slept at all and I couldn't eat, which under less stressful situations would have been my way of coping, but now my feelings were larger than life and food was the last thing I wanted.

I continually worried that Frosty would be thinking I had abandoned him and that I wasn't coming back. I prayed constantly that he would know I was right outside. I hurt knowing he was hurting and at a time when he needed me most I wasn't there.

The morning did ease some of the fear, knowing the vet and staff were all there. I made up a little song about Frosty coming home today and, when I wasn't singing that, I was praying, talking with my girlfriend in Arizona, and writing affirmations. It felt as though I was in a meditative state most of the time. When I closed my eyes, I could see Frosty and take myself there mentally with him, telling him I was there, hoping he could feel me there.

The day was long and the night was even longer, even more so for Frosty who did not know what was going on or if I was coming back. Or did he know?

I forced myself to stay positive, but of course the fear was always there. My biggest fear was that he would pass in the vet's office without me being able to bring him home again. I thought about that a hundred times a day. I also thought that I didn't want to be the one to decide it was his time. I was insistent that if it was, he would go by God's hands. Of course any time thoughts like that came up, I pushed them back, but they did come up often.

∾ CHAPTER 7 ∾

*S*aturday morning, I counted the minutes to when the vet's office would open and I could call and hear the vet say Frosty was well now and that I could come get him. The vet was in surgery when I called, so I had to wait to talk with him. I was really frustrated with not being able to visit Frosty while he was in the hospital, so, while I waited, I called a few other offices to find out what their policy was. They all said the owner could visit, but that it was hard on the animals because they would bark, scream, and cry, and it created more stress when their owner left. I understood that, thinking, *Well, then, I won't leave Frosty until it's time for him to come home.* I knew that wasn't possible, but it helped to tell myself that. When it's a family member or a friend, for the most part, we have the option of staying with them. This was harder. I couldn't explain it to Frosty, not that explaining would have made any of this any easier.

Around one, I went over to the vet's office to talk with him face to face to get a better feel for what was really going on and if he felt that it was indeed Frosty's time to release his body. The vet said his eyes were good but he still was too dizzy to stand. He wanted to keep him until Monday. He said that was his advice but that I could do what I wanted; it was my decision. I could see the men in little white coats coming for me. My frustration and fear were now turning to anger. I wanted to blame someone and throw all this emotion at someone. The vet was an obvious choice since he was standing right in front of me. I insisted he go over the blood test results again with me, even though he already had. They had shown very little, nothing really except things mostly due to normal aging. In fact for Frosty's age, things looked really good. I asked why I couldn't take him home and have a technician come by and check on the IV. He said that wasn't a good idea. I had some medical background, so having Frosty at home with the IV was not a concern for me—at least he would be at home.

I went outside for a few minutes to collect my thoughts. My gut was telling me not to take him home, especially if a couple more days would clear things up and Frosty would be better. If I took him home too soon and then had to bring him back again, that would be even harder on us both. I knew before I could agree to leave him there through Monday that I would need to see him to decide for myself. I talked the vet into letting me see Frosty and we agreed that, if he didn't cry and carry on and get too wound up, the vet would let me come back again on Sunday. I asked if there were going to be other dogs there over the weekend and if someone was there full time to take care of the animals. He answered my questions and then I ran home to get some of the food Frosty was familiar with.

When I came back, the vet walked me back right away to where Frosty was. I knew I would have to contain myself from climbing in the cage and holding him or dragging him out and taking him home. As I knelt down next to Frosty's cage, he sensed someone was there, but he looked at me as if he couldn't see. I am sure he thought it was someone from the vet coming to him. It took him only a second before he realized it was me and he started to pull his legs in to stand up. I opened the cage and grabbed him to keep him from standing. Yes, I did want to climb in with him. I was so relieved that he knew me and that he did seem better to me. I tried to stay calm, so he would stay calm, but it was hard. He started to whine just a little and I could feel the tears coming on.

I handed him the food, which he wanted nothing to do with. He just wanted me. I was glad the vet had left the room so I could be alone with Frosty. I told him his angels were here, which he probably already knew. I told him Faye, my girlfriend who had transitioned thirty years before, was there with him. I was sure he knew that too. He looked at me in a way that made it seem as if he was looking above me, and I wondered if he was looking at his guardian angel. I reached farther into the cage so that I could hug him, and he wagged his tail and inched forward on his stomach, trying to move toward me. Something Frosty had always done with me that was so endearing was when I hugged him, he always bent his head in toward mine and put his paw over my arm. As he did that then, I felt hope and strength raise in me, but when I looked in his eyes I felt fear. He was trying to tell me something. I couldn't let myself think he was telling me it was time for his transition. I had to believe he was telling me, *I'm okay and I know you're here.* I wondered if he thought I didn't love him or didn't want him because he was sick. I desperately wanted to know that he knew I was there for him and that I still wanted him and always would.

I stepped away from the cage a few times, then stepped back again, hoping he would understand that I was leaving but also that I was coming back again. The vet came back in and said it was time to go. All this had happened over a ten-minute period. It felt more like twenty seconds. I had to force myself to leave, was afraid to leave. Would I see him again? I was so afraid he would transition there at the vet's by himself. The vet assured me he would be going home with me. I wondered how Frosty would be when he came home, but of course, however he was would be okay with me. I loved taking care of him, was always honored to take care of him.

I stood out in the hall, listening to see if Frosty would cry and get too wound up when I left. It took him a couple of minutes and he did start to whine and cry, not as badly as some but clearly it would be better for him if I wasn't coming and then leaving him again.

I wanted to stay, badly I wanted to stay, yet there was a part of me that wanted to run. I was afraid of what I had seen, afraid of what I was feeling, and afraid of what Frosty was going through. Working as a psychic, I had seen all those things before. It was strange how very different it seemed and how really different it felt now. I wanted to hold on to Frosty and never let him go, and there was that part of me that wanted to run from the panic and the fear and that voice in my heart that kept trying to tell me something. The vet said it wasn't Frosty's time and not to worry: he would be going home on Monday. My friends, the few that I told, all said the same thing: it was not his time. If it wasn't his time, why couldn't I shake this panic that kept threatening to choke me? I wanted to believe what they were saying so I clung to it, but that little voice in my head wouldn't go away. I drowned it out with affirmations and positive thinking, but all the while I never stopped to notice I had begun the grieving process. That little voice said that I just wanted to get him home, that if he was going to transition into spirit, then I wanted him home. I wanted to be with him and I wanted God to make the decision—not me, not the vet, but God.

The rest of Saturday was long, so very long, and I wondered what was going on in Frosty's mind. I thought of the families I had worked with throughout the years, one in particular that had been through the same thing with their son. I now fully understood their grief, their shock, and the paralyzing thoughts that come with trying to cope with this kind of thing. The looks I had seen on their faces were now on mine. Mentally I was wearing down.

I knew Frosty needed to be on the IV and I hadn't wanted to run the risk of taking him home too soon, but I couldn't help but wonder if this was really going to work. I knew I would need more support. I called my chiropractor. He and his wife had worked on Frosty and me for years. They were expanded function, in that they had more education, certification, and training than the normal chiropractor. They both spent time talking with me and doing adjustments on me to help my body release all the emotion that was going on. The reiki master from Arizona who had been working on Frosty stepped up his efforts as well, not only working on Frizz, but me too. I began to feel calmer, and hearing them all say it wasn't his time helped the calm to settle the panic. All of this was really tough, but I also knew that God had his own plan and trusting that plan right now was one of the hardest things I had ever had to do. It was something I had not been very good at in the past. I stayed in the parking lot until I was sure the police were going to come and cite me for camping there, and then I forced myself to go home.

Sunday, I knew, would be long and for Frosty even longer. I had brought him there and left him and now the vet had left him too. Frosty liked being around people, so I wondered about the quiet of the place, without people coming and going. I kept talking to him in my mind, just like I always had, praying he could hear me. He had always seemed like he could hear me in the past so I had no reason to doubt that he could hear me now, except that my fear kept trying to convince me otherwise.

I took a quick shower, loaded up the van with whatever I thought I might need—mostly Frosty's things—and headed once again to the vet's parking lot. I just wanted to be near Frizz; I wanted to be sure someone was there with him. As the day wore on, it got harder. I knew someone was there, but I didn't know how Frosty was. My girlfriend in Arizona said a veterinary employee would call me if anything came up. I clung to that, but it didn't change that panic in me. I did the usual praying, writing thousands of affirmations, and singing the little songs that I had made up. I talked to Frosty constantly in my head and in prayer, visualizing me being there with him, next to him.

At times I lost it and cried my heart out, giving way to the grief of deep down knowing what was happening. I wrote letters to God and talked with him, telling him this was more than I could handle. I had already been through some major losses in my life and this one was just too much. I begged God to give me more time—six months, a year, just more time—in which Frosty's health would be good and we could go to the park and do all the things that we had always done. I got mad at God and I begged God, screaming at him, telling him I could not, *would not,* do this. I couldn't lose Frosty and definitely not like this.

After crying for an hour, I would force myself to focus on love, to see the gifts in this and try hard to embrace it. I was able to do that early in the day, but the later it got, the more tired I got and the angrier I felt. I wanted to know what kind of God would do this, like this. He had made Frosty and me both and he had connected us in this way, so why take him through so much pain? *Heal him, and then take him peacefully in old age.* I wanted no part of God's plan, or what I was thinking was his plan. I knew it was the fear talking, but, at that point, I couldn't help it. I didn't want to help it.

As night came, my girlfriend Shelley, who was in Arizona, helped me to see that I needed God on my side right now, so I had to deal with the anger and move on. I shifted into a softer version of begging him to bring Frosty home now. Calming down, getting into a quieter mode of begging, did help me to focus more and talk to Frosty. I begged him to hang in there and to know I was there with him. I felt angels and I knew his angels were with him. I hoped they were his healing angels and not his angels of transition. I just had to assume—no, *believe*—he was okay, that he was home now.

⧼ CHAPTER 8 ⧽

*M*onday morning the vet's office opened at 8:00 a.m. I called at 8:01. I had to wait for the doctor to come out of surgery to talk with him. It was mind boggling.

At 11:00 a.m., I was ready to head over there and scream, "Give me back my Frizzy." I clearly was hanging on the edge by the time the vet called, but he did call with great, great news! Frizzy was coming home! I was laughing and crying and trying to stay calm all at once. The vet said he would like to keep him until three o'clock, to keep him on the IV as long as possible, but that he could definitely come home that day. The vet said Frosty still wasn't eating all that well. I knew that would change as soon as I got him home. I wondered how he would be and more importantly how he would feel. I knew he would feel better at home, but how stable would he be? The vet had said he could stand but that he wasn't real stable on his own and that I would need to be with him. That was no problem. I had put work on hold

41

and for me the important thing was getting Frosty well. I could hardly wait to put my arms around him and look into his eyes and see how he really was. I started praying that he would understand why I hadn't been there and that I wanted him and I wanted him home no matter what. I couldn't bear to think that he might think I didn't want him, or that I didn't love him.

My heart was pounding as we pulled up to the vet's office. My older son, the one who had carried him in, was there to carry him out. The vet had said he could walk but that he wasn't stable. I was thinking I would just have my son carry him out, to get him in the van. I wanted to run ahead and hug Frosty and tell him he was going home and I would never let him go. I forced myself to go slowly and stay calm.

My son went in with the vet to get Frosty—we figured Frosty might get too excited seeing me and our intention was to keep him calm as much as possible. I watched from the back as my son started coaxing Frosty toward the door of the cage. He stood on his own but needed help stepping out as the cage was elevated. As my son reached to help Frosty out, Frosty must have sensed me there, because he stopped and looked up, making eye contact with me. I couldn't stand back anymore. I called his name as I stepped forward and his tail wagged and he came to life. His energy shifted. It was like courage, strength, and joy rolled in to give him life.

I fought back the tears and threw my arms around him and lifted him out, with my son's help of course. Once in the van I felt hopeful that he was going to be okay. My son lifted Frosty and set him on the floor and then climbed in to hold him. Frosty was used to lying on the couch and to the couch he was headed. My son grabbed him and sat with him on the floor, which for the moment seemed like a less strenuous thing for Frosty, but Frizz was on cloud nine! He was coming home!

Once home in the driveway, we put Frosty's harness back on him and my son lifted him out and set him on the front lawn. It was like he'd never left. I had a hold of the harness, but Frosty was actually walking on his own. I breathed a sigh of relief as I let go of the lead. He really could walk on his own. This was so much better than I had thought it would be.

When he was done with his business, he headed back to the front door and I quickly grabbed his leash and we walked into the house. I opened the door to the bedroom and in he walked. My family and I had put a big spa box in the bedroom just in case I needed to leave him for a few minutes, which wasn't likely, but I wanted to be sure he was safe if I did have to. He was doing so well, better then I had hoped, but the vet had warned me that he might be unstable for a while.

Frosty made it clear right off the bat that he was going to have nothing to do with the box. He walked over and plopped down in front of his big window and looked out. He gave a big sigh of relief and laid his head down. He was home.

I decided not to feed him right away, but I wanted to make sure he had water so I grabbed a small bowl and a bottle of water and offered him some. Since our early days when we would run in the park, I would take a bottle of water that we would share. Frosty got used to drinking from the bottle—yeah, I know he was a little spoiled, but on our runs I always wanted to make sure he had enough water. I was fine, great actually, with giving it to him this way now too. I was so very grateful to have him home so it was fine with me to be holding the bowl for him now.

He fell asleep after the water and I sat and stared at him, trying not to crowd or smother him. Watching him breathe was a gift. I had spent so much time in grief and now to have so much joy was something I intended to hold onto and cherish. Needless to say, we both slept on the floor that night and many other nights as well.

In the morning, Frosty seemed even better. I walked next to him holding his leash, but he was doing so well; he was close to not needing me next to him at all, but I was going for the more cautious approach. I had put rugs down on all the floors to give him sturdier footing for going back and forth to the backyard. He was doing so much better than I thought he would be at this point. He had lost weight over the last four days, since he hadn't been eating very well. I started out feeding him small meals four and five times a day, in small portions to get his stomach used to having food in it. He always ate everything I gave him, which meant he would begin to fill out quickly and feel better.

We spent the next day being very low keyed, staying at home, and I stayed glued to his side. I loved being with him and he was eating and drinking and even held one of his beloved stuffed friends in his mouth when I put it in front of him. He didn't move around a lot, but I expected he would be tired. He had been through a lot. I continued to pour him water from the water bottle, holding a bowl underneath his mouth while I poured the water in front of him. He seemed to like it more this way and he drank more with me bringing it to him. The medication he was taking I stuffed into pill pockets so he took all of it with ease, and I was grateful for that.

In the afternoon, we ventured into the walk-in shower and I gave him a sponge bath. He liked the warm water spraying on him; it always made his hips feel better. The shower was big enough for him to lie in so he didn't get too tired. Frosty, being a retriever, always loved the water but was never too thrilled about a shower. He would rather play in the beach or lake or even the sprinklers, but once in the shower he seemed to enjoy it.

That night we both slept again on the floor and it went well. I left a little light on in case he got up to move around—I could get to him more quickly without it being so dark.

The next morning, Frosty climbed up on the bed! A few months prior, I had switched to a special box spring to lower the bed, making it easier for Frosty to get up and down. He loved to be up there in the center, sprawled out like he owned the place, and I always loved seeing him up there. On this morning, I ran out to the kitchen to grab his medicine.

I still wasn't leaving him alone for more than a minute, and when I came back, there he was lying in the center of the bed. He was looking toward the door, with his big brown eyes waiting to hear me squeal, "Frizzy!" when I walked in and saw him on the bed, which of course I did. I knelt down next to him and asked, "How did you do that?" We were both so thrilled and I knew he was giving me a gift.

I took him for a short walk that day to the neighbor's driveway and back. He seemed so much better, and I had hopes of maybe taking him to the park on Saturday or Sunday.

As I mentioned earlier, I had been taking Frosty to a holistic chiropractor for the last few years. With all the jumping up and down off beds and into the van, I wanted to keep his back and hips as healthy as possible. It worked out well that my chiropractor also loved and worked with animals. Frosty loved going and he loved the doctor, and he really loved all the Scooby snacks and that the doctor talked to him as if he were a real person, someone important. Frosty would stand up and watch out the window until he saw him coming to the van, and then he would jump down off the seat and bark as if telling him to hurry. Frosty was a little less energetic on that day, but he knew where he was and he was happy to be there. I had been a little concerned about taking him, as it was a twenty-minute drive to the doctor's office, but his breathing actually seemed better than it had been in months. The visit went well and Frosty seemed even better after that. I was starting to think maybe this all was just an infection and it was going to clear up and everything really was going to be okay. I wanted to believe it, so why did I feel like I was always on pins and needles?

On Thursday Frosty again wanted to be up on the bed, and this time I was there to help him up. His balance was a lot better but still a little off, so I was being overprotective. I loved seeing Frosty up on the bed. He was always so proud of being up there and even more proud when I cheered him on and he would do that endearing wink with his right eye. The wink was something Frosty had started doing about eight or nine years earlier. He would wink just like a person winks at you. I spent time over those years trying to catch it on video, but I never was able to. I never knew when he was going to do it and he never gave any advanced warning, so not only did I never get it on camera, but no one else ever saw him do it. It was one of those things that was between him and me, but it made me laugh when he did it.

On that same day, Frosty lay down on his left side to take his nap. That was something he had not done for six or seven months. He had been lying mostly on his stomach to sleep. I was thrilled to see it and again so amazed at how well he was doing. I was mostly glad that he seemed so much more comfortable in his body than he had been in a while.

We continued our walks every day. Some days he would go a little farther, other days he didn't seem to want to go at all. I would let him decide how fast and how far he would go. I knew how much he loved being outside, feeling the sun, so we would sit outside under the tree on our blanket. Frosty would look around, sniffing, which I loved to watch because his nose would twitch like a bunny rabbit and it would make me laugh. I would ask him if he smelled chicken. He would stop sniffing and look at me—well, *stare* at me—wait a minute, and then start sniffing again. That would make me laugh harder, which would bring a second look from Frizz, with him saying, "I am doing much more important things than sniffing chicken."

Over Halloween weekend, Frosty seemed as if he was getting stronger. He had begun to gain the weight back and was eating really well. He had been seeing the vet and the chiropractor for weekly checkups, with a thumbs-up each time. He was still on antibiotics, which seemed to be helping. I was of course still praying, writing affirmations, and doing energy work with crystals on him. And Dwayne, the reiki master from Arizona, was working on him too. The chiropractor had given me a crystal pendant that seemed to make an even bigger difference, and Frosty was now wearing that full-time. I continued with the gratitude board, affirmations, and of course asking God every day and every night for Frosty to be now in perfect health. Things were really looking up. The lump in my throat and the knot in my stomach remained, but I was breathing more easily at times and I was beginning to sleep a little bit more each night. I was hoping God had changed his mind and really was going to give me and Frizz more time.

∽ CHAPTER 9 ∽

*I*t was now the first of November, and, up to that point, the only place we had gone was the vet and the chiropractor. It seemed to be hard on Frosty most when he was riding in the van and I didn't want to tire him out, but, on that Monday, it seemed as though he might be ready for more. We hit the vet's office first, receiving the great news that all was going well. It was joyous news and so off we went to do a few long-overdue errands that were right around the house. I considered taking Frosty to the park that day, but I knew getting him in and out would tire him just as much as riding around in the van would. I had started using a ramp three or four years prior, as it was quite a jump for him getting in and out. Using the ramp prevented the impact on his shoulders and hips. It turned out to be good day and Frosty seemed glad that things were getting back to normal.

Tuesday went by with the usual walk and lots of hugs and kisses. I still wasn't over having him gone, so, yes, I was still smothering him just a bit and my heart was still not sure which way this was going to go. I had taken time off work and was glad to just be there with Frizz and grateful for the time with him.

The next day, Wednesday, November 3, we had another appointment with the chiropractor. Frosty was going weekly now and his session this week was encouraging. He gobbled up the Scooby snacks and seemed ready for a short walk. There was a big grass area that went around the building, so, after Frosty's checkup, I took him out and we walked for about ten minutes. It doesn't sound like much, but for Frosty it was. He was tired but proud of himself, and I did the normal "Yahoo! Way to go Frizz!" I was thinking we would soon be able to hit the park again.

On Thursday a friend, who probably will grow up to be a chef, came by to cook up fresh vegetables and meat for Frosty. Yes, he was (and will always be) one spoiled pup. He loved the home cooking and he loved the chef, so it was a fun day for Frizz. He found the strength to stand in the kitchen for as long as it took for the small crumbs to land on the floor or for his friend to give him some, whichever came first. When he got tired, he lay on the blanket we'd put on the floor, so he could be in the kitchen with us, while all the cooking was going on. Frosty was tired at the end of the day, but he'd eaten well and it still seemed as if he was improving.

Friday brought more reason to cheer. Frosty, with the help of one of my closest friends and one of Frizz's favorite people, made it even farther on our neighborhood walk. My girlfriend who lives a few houses away came out to her mailbox and stood out on the sidewalk, cheering him on. He was used to getting treats from her so when he saw her, he trotted on down to her house like he was a young pup! It was fun for all of us and I think, for the moment, Frosty forgot that there was anything going on in his physical body. For the moment, he was outside in the sun, with the trees and he was trotting and happy and feeling great. We all laughed and celebrated Frizz!

My focus and my goal daily were still on taking Frosty to the park. He still tired easily but he seemed to be getting better, or so I thought. I was afraid to push it, as getting him in and out of the van and then walking there was a lot. I could see he was in pain somewhere in his body. Of course Frizz would have said, "Let's go." I was the one afraid of him getting too tired, or maybe I was afraid if we went it would be the last time we went. Maybe I was afraid of what I would know.

I was loving our time together even though we did stay at home. I loved the quiet of the nighttime, with just him and me. When the house would get quiet and everyone went to bed, it was like angels filled our room. It was beautiful and serene. I still slept on the floor with him as much as I could, but it was getting colder and Frosty's breathing was better with the windows open, so some nights I had to shift to the bed to stay warm. On the nights I slept on the bed, Frosty always slept up against the side of the bed, next to me. I would sleep with my hand on him, so if he moved I would know it. The big box that had been put in the bedroom for his return home had been removed. I'd only used it once and Frosty hadn't liked it.

∾ CHAPTER 10 ∾

*T*he second week of November took us to another recheck with the vet and a change in antibiotics, but all still seemed to be going well as far as the vet was concerned. For me, I wasn't too sure. It was at about that time that Frosty started sleeping more and more next to the window instead of next to the bed. It was like he was pulling away just a little bit more again. At first, I of course took it personally, but deep down I knew. I found myself at times hugging him and sobbing. I still wouldn't or couldn't admit to myself or anyone what I knew, but the level of grief I was feeling spoke for itself. I had stepped just a little deeper into the process of grief, which I had already begun months before when we had taken our trip to Utah. There really was no denying then what was to come, but I was still so resistant to going there in any way. I'm sure it made it harder on Frosty, because of course he did know. He had been working at easing the pain of separation for months now, working at it gradually since April. I had turned a blind eye to it then, just as I still was months later. I put on a tunnel vision of him being around another year or so. Oh, I knew he wouldn't be around forever, but when you spend every day with someone for that long, whether it's a person or a furry friend, it's hard.

I decided to hold on to the fact that he was going to go when I was ready. He was only a couple of months away from his birthday—of course he would be here for that, I kept telling myself. I refused to give in to the thoughts that were there in my head and beginning to scream louder. All my friends were still saying, "No way, not his time," and it was easy to stick with that because that is what I wanted to believe and that is what I wanted to hear. I desperately wanted to believe them, so I did. I blocked out my own gut and all the signs that were coming to me.

Shortly after the grief became more apparent, I started having panic attacks. I would get shaky and hear the same sentence over and over in my head. It kept saying, "I just need to hear my own voice." It kept coming and it got louder as each day progressed. Finally I pulled out some old affirmation tapes I had recorded in my own voice and began listening to them. The voice in my head softened just a bit but never really went away. The fear, however, was so much louder that it wasn't until weeks later I realized what the voice had been trying to tell me: to listen to my own voice, because my own voice knew, *really knew*, the truth about Frosty.

A few months prior to all this happening, I had scheduled the carpets throughout the house to be cleaned. I considered canceling. I wanted things calm for Frizz and I didn't want to give up time with him, plus the voice inside my head said, *You like the doggie smell and the dog hair. What if it was gone?* I shut the voice up, telling it to stop thinking such thoughts. I decided to let the guy come and do just the walkways of the carpet, not moving any furniture. When the guy came, I immediately felt uncomfortable, my inner voice screaming at me the whole time, but lately I had gotten used to blocking out my own voice so I held my breath and let him do it. I kept thinking and worrying about how the chemicals would be for Frosty: if it would be too much for him. The guy assured me it wouldn't hurt us or the dog. I loaded Frosty into the van when it was time to shampoo our room. I had scheduled a recheck with the vet and the chiropractor, so we would be out of the house for a few hours, giving the carpet time to dry and air out before we returned.

The checkup with the vet went really well. In fact, we decided Frosty could go two weeks before the next checkup. I was elated and we headed off to the chiropractor to give him the good news! At the chiropractor again there were more Scooby snacks and a good visit and more hope. Everything was going so well, so why was I feeling so uneasy and fighting off crying all the time? I was sticking to Frosty like glue and canceling anything that took me away from him. Everything could wait, I keep thinking, I just wanted to be with Frizz. He was eating okay and drinking plenty—I was making sure of that. I was still pouring him water from the bottle. He was doing so well, everyone was saying, but why then wasn't that overwhelming feeling of panic going away or at least easing up?

As soon as we got back to the house, I opened windows, turned on fans, and ran the allergen remover in the bedroom. I could smell just a slight odor but nothing too strong, so I thought it would be okay. I left windows open that night, just in case.

The next morning I was still holding my breath and still not sure I had done the right thing in having the carpets shampooed; it was obviously too late now, but I was still second-guessing myself.

Later in the day, Frosty started acting just slightly different. I was always so in tune to him that I couldn't even tell you what it was, I just felt something different in him. I thought maybe going to the vet and the chiropractor all in one day might have been too much, or could it have been the carpets? By evening I started feeling weird too. Working as a psychic, sometimes you pick up on and feel when others are sick, so I wasn't sure at first if it was me or Frosty feeling sick from the carpets or something else. I just knew I was feeling something. It felt similar to having a slight case of the flu. I again thought about the carpets and decided I better put a sheet down for Frosty to sleep on, so he wasn't sleeping directly on the carpet. Deciding it was the smell from the chemicals that was bothering him, I ragged on myself again for having it done.

∽ CHAPTER 11 ∾

On Friday morning, Frosty refused to eat. It was the first time he had rejected his food since coming home from the hospital three weeks ago. It sent me into a bigger panic than I had already been in. I started blaming myself for having the carpets done and how stupid I was: he had been doing so well. I thought, *Now we we're back to square one and having to start over.* The panic was overwhelming. It was hard to think, and staying calm was nowhere near what I was feeling or able to think. Was it really the carpets that had created this relapse, or was it my fear and panic of him not being fine now that was now manifesting itself in him? The fear was pushing me into guilt mode, which I knew better. I just felt so panicked and so scared. I actually was feeling sick myself, but I wasn't sure if I was feeling what was going on inside of Frizz or if it was my emotions or if it was from the carpets. I wanted to believe it was the carpets. Of course I wanted to believe he was going to be okay, but the panic once again was overriding any rational thoughts I was having.

We stayed outside a lot that day, keeping him in the fresh air. He lay on his blanket and did the little sniffy thing with his nose. I called the shampoo company, asking for a new referral for someone new to come back to rinse the carpets with no chemicals. I was really feeling guilty, kicking myself all the way, telling myself not only had this made Frosty relapse, but now his fur and smell was no longer on the carpet.

None of the guilt I was dumping on myself was helping the situation at all, but I just couldn't bring myself to stop. Besides, it gave me a distraction from the panic I was feeling. It just had to be the carpets that were making Frosty feel sick again. It had to be that and nothing else.

I left the doors and windows to the house open all day with the fans blowing. We slept in the bedroom that night, Frosty sleeping on the floor near the window, me on the floor as close to him as he would allow. I was a mess, and I'm sure the way I was feeling wasn't helping him either. I was so busy being crazed that I couldn't be there for him. Our lessons are as difficult as we choose to make them. I was making mine really painful.

When we got up Saturday morning, Frosty was not much better but not any worse either, so that gave me some hope. We again spent most of our time outside, with Frizz lying on his favorite outdoor blanket. My girlfriend brought him down some of his favorite treats and he ate them, which was a great sign. He was trying, I could see that, but something had changed. I had talked with the vet and he said to bring him in on Monday if things weren't any different. Frosty seemed so physically weak, and mentally I was worn out. I decided that we would sleep in the van over the weekend, as it was free of any odors that might be bothering Frosty. Another guy was coming to shampoo carpets on Monday and then all would be well again. I just had to keep telling myself to override that constant voice in my head that kept saying, *Time is running out.*

The thought had come to me briefly that Frosty and I were the only two in the house who seemed to be bothered by the carpet smell. I just had to make myself believe everything was okay and that it would be okay. There was a bright spot to focus on in all this. When Frosty and I slept in the van, it was on a big king-size bed in the back so he slept on the bed with me. It gave me a chance to gently mush him, hug and kiss him, and be close to him again and he didn't seem to mind at all. It was a gift, a gift that helped to get me through. It was also during that time that I knew, really knew. Being that close to him physically again—well, with anyone—you just can't deny it. You *know.* I knew he was going to leave. I could feel it, and, as a result, I found myself—when I could sleep—waking up to tears streaming down my checks. I tried to stop it because I knew Frosty would know, but something told me he too was crying. Words came out that I couldn't stop, words of "I miss you Frizz, and I love you, and I pray you are comfortable in your body now." It was like I was talking in my sleep. I would suddenly wake up and realize he was still there, so I would force myself to believe he was going to be okay. There had been other times throughout the past few months when I would go to sleep crying, knowing, but never admitting to anyone or myself what I knew. I was too afraid to say it out loud.

This human stuff is full of lessons that none of us really want to learn. Whether it's been with a partner, brother, sister, mother, father, or friend, you've been through it and you know the pain and the fear of how I was feeling.

It was Saturday night in the van when I took off my rose quartz necklace that I always wore and put it on Frizz. I felt it would help his breathing and the healing of his heart, and help him go through the things he was going through. I wanted him to have as much strength as possible. It would surround him and me both with love, and it would leave his energy on the rose quartz. I had a strawberry quartz that belonged to Frosty's mother and it had helped him and me with the transition when she released her body a few years earlier.

The weather outside was cold, but with the big blanket we always used it was great to sleep in the van. It'd been awhile since we'd done so, and all the memories of the places we'd been surrounded us each night. I realized how much I'd learned from Frosty and how much I was beginning to really open to love. My heart was hurting—yes, in a big way—but it also was opening to love. I was just so grateful to be sleeping with him and to have the time together.

∾ CHAPTER 12 ∾

Sunday morning, it took Frosty longer than usual to get up. I let him go awhile, but then I encouraged him, and even then he wasn't ready. The bribery of breakfast wasn't working as well as it used to, and even my singing the little song I sang to him in the morning only seemed to get him to lift his head. He still was in no hurry to start his day, so I finally just coaxed him out. I was still able to get him down the ramp and out of the van without too much problem. We went out to the backyard to do his business and then I took him into the bedroom, laying clean sheets on the carpet to separate him from any residue that might still be there. I had left the windows open, and the allergen remover running so the room didn't smell of the carpet cleaner—of course I still wanted to blame it all on the carpets. Frosty wouldn't touch his breakfast and lunch also went by without him eating. I couldn't get him to take any treats, which meant his medicine was not going down either. He would only store the treats in his mouth, as if he was trying to swallow, but they wouldn't go down and in the end he would spit them out. It was like he didn't have any control over his tongue.

We still spent a lot of time outside that day. I had already called the vet, so he knew that we would be going back in first thing in the morning. I was expecting the vet to say he needed to go back on the IV antibiotics, but telling myself that would fix everything and Frosty would be fine kept my thinking positive. I was concerned that not being able to get any of the medicine down him for the last two days would be part of the reason he seemed to have relapsed so quickly, and to such an extreme. I still, even knowing what I knew, wasn't going to go there, not yet, not completely.

Sunday evening we had fresh roasted chicken, hoping that would make Frosty want to eat. It did! When *the chicken* walked in the door, Frosty got up and headed to the kitchen. There was nothing wrong with his nose. We could all see that. He stood in the kitchen begging for the chicken. I wondered if giving it to him would hurt him more than help him. He had a slight allergy to chicken and an even bigger one to beef. I know: how could a dog be allergic to either one? Well everyone who knew him said he was not a dog. That little voice said, *It probably doesn't matter what he eats at this point as long as he eats,* so I gave it to him. He ate all of it and wanted more. I was hopeful. I even got the medicine down him, wrapped in the chicken. The chicken had worked so well, later he got fresh turkey breast, which he ate up too! I felt even more hopeful when it appeared that the chicken and the turkey were staying down. I knew Frosty felt better for having eaten too, and I was grateful for that. We both went to bed feeling much better, me knowing he had eaten and Frosty because he had food in his stomach and the medicine too. I even got a shower while one of the family members sat with Frizz. I'd been grabbing showers here and there when someone was available to sit with him. I just didn't trust leaving him on his own, because he would wander the house looking for me.

When Frosty was a puppy, he would follow me into the bathroom and lie next to the shower door. If I took longer than he wanted me to, he would stand up and push his noise onto the shower door until I opened it. I would open it and splash his face with water, and he would bark and I would laugh. When he got older, he would come in and just lie next to the shower, waiting patiently. Other times he would lie in the bedroom doorway where he could see into the bathroom and know when I was out. *Then* he would come in. Yes, I get that he sounds really spoiled, and he was. He had a lot of love and he gave a lot of love.

That night after my shower, we sat for a while in the weight room. It was the only room that had not been shampooed and it had a big, thick rug he always lay on while I was working out. He had two of his toys and, as he was up to playing, I kept grabbing them from him. He would bark and then I'd give them back. We played the blow-in-your-face game, with him giving me that look out of the corner of his eye. I was gratefully surprised he seemed to be feeling

BETHANY-ELIZABETH FAYE HANSEN

so good. It felt so great to see him playing and to be playing with him; it had been awhile since he seemed this happy and at peace in his body. We stayed in the weight room for about an hour, me writing affirmations and playing with Frizz. He ate a little bit more, and then we went outside to the bathroom and headed for the van. Things felt better than they had in a while. It was easy getting Frizzy up the ramp and into the van and it wasn't too cold. We had the big blanket and each other. Frizz was still wearing my rose quartz and the crystal pendant from the chiropractor, so it felt like being surrounded in peace.

The next morning I woke up dreading going to the vet's office; even with Frosty being so good the night before, I was scared. He seemed a little weaker and, once again, he didn't want to get up.

The vet came out to the van, which had become his usual way to see Frosty. It just made things easier on me and Frizz. He took a minute to exam him and then he said, "It doesn't look good." Frizz was really low on oxygen. My heart jumped to my throat with fear and thoughts of what I could do for him. He had no fever, but the vet wanted to take him inside to do a more detailed exam. I felt scared and panicked and I was praying for angels to be with Frizz. Here it was again: him not feeling good and me leaving him. I always wondered what he was thinking. Why is it that we seem to be forced to leave our loved ones at the worst possible times?

Once again, I was removing his harness, the rose quartz, and the crystal pendant. Frosty was shaking as I am sure all of our loved ones do when they are feeling what Frosty was feeling. The vet said to come back in two hours. He wanted to do another EKG, a chest X-ray, and some more blood work. I raced home, grabbed a few things, my writing pad, a few CDs, and headed right back to my now familiar spot in the parking lot. I started counting the minutes until I could go in and get Frosty. I was in a place of *this is enough* and I was feeling angry—yes, some of it toward God. My ego really wanted to scream out, *Just give him back to me!* Once again, I found myself fighting the anger and the feelings of wanting to blame someone.

An hour and a half went by and I had waited long enough, so I headed in to get my sweet Frizz and to see the results of the testing. The vet went over them all, showing me first the X-rays, and they showed the usual results: things didn't look too bad. He said they actually looked pretty good for Frosty's age. He said the blood tests would be back in the morning and the EKG seemed normal except for the breathing being labored. He said I could take him home, but that he would start him on a different antibiotic. They brought my sweet, precious Frizzy out to me, and as soon as Frosty saw me he wagged his tail, saying, "Wow, Mama, I didn't expect to see you so soon." Seeing his tail wag was so wonderful for me. I hurried over and hugged him, grabbing his leash and heading out to go home. It was then I decided, tired or not, right or wrong, we would go to the park tomorrow, first thing in the morning. Today we had another appointment with the chiropractor and I didn't want to tire him out too much.

We hurried home to meet with my girlfriend before the chiropractic appointment. She was coming over to get some pictures of Frizz and me. I didn't have very many of him and me together, and I wanted to get some more. That little voice had been screaming at me to get them done.

Pulling in the driveway, my heart was so full with gratitude for having Frosty home with me. I just kept looking at him and trying to soak in everything about him. I walked him carefully down his ramp and over to the grass so he could go to the bathroom. I stayed close, just in case he seemed wobbly. He'd been through another long day and it was only one in the afternoon, but he was doing great. It was strange how much stronger he seemed than when I'd taken him to the vet this morning. It almost made me forget how he had been over the last few days.

∽ CHAPTER 13 ∽

Frosty was still on the lawn when I reached over to grab something from the van, and, as I turned back toward him, I was only about ten feet from him when he did it. He stopped walking toward me, looked up at me, directly into my eyes, and he barked five or six times in a row. It was like he was saying something to me. The thought that came to me was that Angelic, Frosty's mom, had done the same thing five days before she had released her body. The thought was so quick and I dismissed it just as quickly. I was feeling hopeful and he seemed so good that he had to be doing better. It was a clenched, tight dismissal that left me with that usual panic. He had to be better; he had just barked at me as if he was nine or ten years old. He had to be better; he could not be dying, not my Fizzy. I walked over and wrapped my arms around him and said, "What are you trying to tell me?" He looked confused; usually I knew what he was saying. I grabbed his short leash that he now wore and walked him into the house and into our bedroom. He was so glad to be home. My girlfriend came down and we spent about thirty minutes taking pictures of Frosty and me together and some of just him. I felt so sad the whole time we were taking the pictures. It just felt like we were saying good-bye.

I look at the pictures now and wonder how I could not have admitted what was really happening. I feel guilt because I didn't listen to my heart. If I had, things would have been different for Frosty in his transition. Yes, I do feel guilty and yes, I do feel angry with myself. I should have admitted it to myself; I should have listened to him and to me. I was too scared, too focused on what I thought I was losing.

When we were done taking the pictures, I loaded Frosty back into the van so we could go to his chiropractor appointment. My girlfriend was walking down the driveway as I got into the van. I headed back to Frizz to make sure he was okay. I watched as Frosty raised his head to watch her go. I knocked on the window, and she came back and waved at him. Again that little voice said, *He's saying good-bye to her.* It was so painful to feel and to watch that I just couldn't grasp it. I pushed it all back with the quick thought of, *We have to get to the park.*

I shut the van door, flipped on the ignition switch, and cried all the way to the chiropractor. I wanted to feel hopeful. I wanted to believe that if Frosty was going to go, God would take him while Frosty and I were together. Nothing had showed on the tests, so I pushed myself to hold on to that thought. This had to be just a little setback, but it wasn't his time. My ego said *Yes, don't ask, because you don't want to know.* I forced myself to believe that we would have Thanksgiving and my birthday together. It wasn't his time.

The chiropractic appointment went well and the house was clearing out, but the thought kept coming to me to sleep in the van one more night. A new guy was coming the next day to rinse the carpets again, so all would be well after that.

I got someone to sit with Frizz and I took a quick shower and then again hung out in the weight room. He was in rare form that night too, just as he had been the night before, playing all the games with me we always played. We mushed and blew in the face and he squeezed his toys till they honked, which he always loved to do. We headed out to the van and he actually seemed really good. Of course my head kept reminding me that Angelic had been like this before she passed. I could see Frosty was weaker by the time he lay down in the van, but he still seemed happy. He had eaten some dinner, not much, which made getting the medicine down him somewhat difficult, and I worried about that, but there seemed to be some peace, a peace I wasn't ready to acknowledge the reasoning for. We went to sleep that night feeling that peace and yet there were tears running down my face. I had my hand on Frosty's paw and was feeling the peace, yet I was crying. All this was so confusing. I felt that intense fear come over me.

I sang him one of his songs and tried to stay calm for his sake. I was thinking that Frosty deserved to feel the peace and to know that I was okay, and I wanted that for him too. He was the one going through all this. I was supposed to be there supporting him, but it seemed like it was the other way around.

The next morning, as it had been for the last couple of mornings, Frosty didn't want to get up. I could see he was weaker than the day before. Clearly something was wrong. I let him lie in the van while I ran back and forth getting clothes and getting ready for the new carpet guy to come. I had decided that when he was done, Frizz and I would go hang out in the park. I tried giving Frosty food and water, but he wouldn't take either. The carpet guy came to re-rinse the carpets and it was then that the vet called. He said the blood tests showed that Frosty's pancreas was extremely infected and it was important to get him back on the IV antibiotics. I asked, "Why do it again if the infection is back after doing it before?" He said this time Frosty would not be allowed to eat during the treatment as it had to be only the IV, with nothing else going through his system.

We discussed the pros and cons of putting him back in or not putting him back in. I asked my usual hundred questions and then I asked the vet if he thought it was Frosty's time. He said he didn't think so, but no one but God knew for sure. I told him I would think about everything and get back to him. I didn't want to give up any more time with Frosty. Yet if this would make him better, we would have more time. Back and forth my brain bounced. This was a hard decision, one I had never imagined myself having to make.

I was feeling so much emotion and so many different ones; it was hard to think clearly at all. I was also beginning to lose faith in a God that I had hoped would create miracles, and it didn't seem like he wasn't doing that. It was back and forth, up and down. Just when I thought things were better, they would get worse, or at least it seemed like that.

I hung up the phone with feelings of *What do I do now?* I called the few friends who I had told what was going on and asked what they thought. Everyone said it was not his time. One said, "You have told God what you could handle. Release it to him." Well I felt like I couldn't handle any of this, yet God was still giving it to me. I was starting to feel more anger toward God. I wanted desperately to believe God was going to make Frosty strong and healthy again and that everything was going to be okay. I wanted to believe that it wasn't his time, yet somewhere inside that voice was screaming, *I need to hear the sound of my own voice! I need to hear me!* And yet I didn't want to hear me. I kept shutting it out.

Frosty was pretty weak, but I wanted to get him to the park; it was like going home for us, and I wanted him to be there and the thought had not let up so we went. Once at the park I decided giving Frosty a chance with the antibiotics was something I should do. I would give it until Saturday and then I was bringing him home, no matter what, and this would be the last time. I was worried that if I didn't try it and it could have made a difference, I couldn't live with that. Of course, if it didn't work, that would bother me, too, giving up the time with him. This was about him, so I came to the conclusion that I would do it, praying it would make him better. I was so overly focused on making him better that it never occurred to me to ask, in prayer or of God, if there was anything else about this situation that was important for me to know. I didn't want to know. I had turned away from knowing. I chose to look at the knowing as painful and unwanted.

∽ CHAPTER 14 ∾

*W*hen we got to the park, we sat in the van for quite a while before getting out. I didn't want to move. I was afraid to move, if I did, it would all end here. I just wanted to hold on to the moment. I just wanted to be with Frizz—you know, stop time. Looking at him was hard, I could see he was in pain and it was hard for him to breathe. Finally I took him down the ramp and out to the park. We loved being in the park with the trees and the bluebirds and the sun, and this park had a really big lake. This was the same park where Faye and I had spent our last visit together before she released her physical body.

Frosty, even though he'd been so weak, started walking. It was like he couldn't decide which way he wanted to go, and once he started he wanted to keep walking. That could have been a sign to me, but I choose to cover it up with the sadness. I was concerned about tiring him out, so I kept trying to lead him back toward the van, not wanting him to walk too far from it, but he would pull away. He would walk a little and then stop and look around and then walk some more. I watched him, finally getting quiet in my own head. Watching him, I could see he was memorizing the park, the way it looked, the trees and the water, studying it. He would look and then walk some more and then stop and look around and study everything even harder. I wanted to stay forever, and he clearly did too. Was he thinking the same things I was? Was he able to take in what was happening? I could take things in only for a few seconds at a time, but then the denial blanketed and blocked any thoughts of him transitioning.

Another ten minutes went by with Frosty still wanting to walk. The vet had stressed how important it was to get Frosty in as soon as possible in order to get him started on the IV. I wasn't ready to leave, probably would never be, and Frosty wasn't ready either. We stayed another ten minutes with him continuing to walk, stop, and memorize until finally he allowed me to coax him back toward the van. I wanted to stay forever and pretend none of this was happening, but it was and he was getting so tired. I didn't want to make things worse, and it was hard seeing him like that. My human mind kept saying, *Just get the IV started as soon as possible and Frosty will be okay.*

I scanned the park myself one more time, taking a mental picture with him in it, and then I walked Frizz up the ramp, getting him into the van and onto the couch in the back. I sat with him for a long time, promising to bring him back to the park on Sunday when he was better. It took me about an hour before I could force myself to leave the park and head to the vet's office. I cried and Frosty was quiet, but along with that was a strange sense of peace that everything was going to be okay.

When we got to the vet's office, I went in first to talk with him again, to ask a few more questions and to be sure of my decision. I told him I would let Frosty stay only until Saturday morning, and, whether he was better or not at that time, I was taking him home no matter what. I went back out to the van to get Frizz. I was feeling as though I was walking into a dark tunnel, not knowing what was at the end. Why was I feeling so much peace if this was the wrong decision?

Frosty was waiting for me, visibly upset: should I be asking him what he wanted? I never thought to do that. I don't know why. In the past it would have been normal for me to ask Frizz, but this time maybe all the fear was too overwhelming. Or maybe I wasn't supposed to ask him this time. I don't know, but I didn't think to, and yes there was guilt because I didn't. I walked Frosty down the ramp one last time, but of course I didn't know that then. I had always prayed to God that when Frosty's time came, it would be God taking him and he would transition him at home. I always clung to that, trying hard to create my own outcome.

Walking him in the door to the vet, he tugged harder than usual. He didn't want to go in. I fought the urge to walk him back out, to leave and say I changed my mind. I figured it was the pain of separation that was causing my fear and my panic to rise.

The vet had me take off Frosty's harness, my rose quartz necklace, and the crystal pendant that he had been wearing. As I took off the pendant, I felt something. It was hard to identify what that feeling was, but it felt like Frosty suddenly got weaker, like he had slipped away, somehow. I slipped the rose quartz over my head and bent down to hold Frosty. The vet had me walk in front of Frosty so he would walk into the room where he was to be treated for the next few days.

Was I doing the right thing? Why again was I doing this? If it was the right thing, why was my heart screaming so loudly and how come I couldn't hear Frizz? I wanted to scream and inwardly of course I was. I was blocking out my own voice, the one I needed to hear. The pain was unbearable, but I forced myself to believe that everything was going to be okay and Frosty would be home and we'd have more time. I bent down one last time, reminding Frosty of my promise that I would be back on Saturday and on Sunday we would go to the park. I told him that, no matter what, I would keep that promise to him. *Please, please, please just get better.*

I couldn't believe this was happening again, that I was having to leave him again. How much strength did God think I had? How much did he think Frosty could bear? Couldn't God see that this was beyond what we could do? What about that saying that God never gives you more than you can handle? Was that all a lie? It had to be, because I couldn't handle this. I had lost other people in my life in the past, but this was beyond any pain I could imagine. Why were we going through this, why was it happening like this?

I forced myself to walk out to the van, but I couldn't leave for hours. I never knew a human being could cry so hard or for so long. How did people get through so much pain? I thought of those who were raising small children and had bills to pay, and suddenly doing it without a partner. I thought about the loss of a child, which I could relate to on a certain level. All that thinking made the tears come harder. I had been journaling since I was twelve and on a daily basis, but this was so very painful that I just couldn't open or even touch my journal now. I was too frozen and too scared, and the idea of the words sticking out there on the pages, screaming the truth at me, was way more than I could handle. I didn't want the truth. I wanted to know Frosty was going to be okay, that he was going to come home and be better and healthy and we would have more time together with him feeling good.

I was desperate to know that we would be able to go to the park and make one or two more trips to San Diego. Oh my God, this was painful. Why was God letting this happen? Where was the God that was loving and caring and gentle? I was starting to feel angry again. I wanted someone to be angry with, to get away from the grief. I knew I had to force myself to not trade the anger because I was afraid of feeling the grief, but the truth was, I was angry. After all, if there was a God, then where was he and why was he letting things happen like this? I had been asking for his help, telling him

I needed his help, that I couldn't do this, that it was over my limit. I needed him to make Frosty well, right now, this minute. I knew I was losing it, thinking things that were, well-- over the top, but I couldn't help it. I didn't want to help it; it was the grief, the exhaustion, and the fear talking. Why did God make Frosty well last time just to make him go through this again? How much did he think Frosty could do? Didn't he love us?

I stayed in the vet's parking lot again that night until early in the morning. I forced myself to visualize taking Frosty home, hearing the vet say, "He's better now." I felt so panicked and tired that it was hard to stay positive. I kept thinking about Frosty and what he was thinking and feeling. I wondered if he was mad because I had dropped him off again when he clearly had told me not to. Was he wondering if I loved him? It was hard to even pray, let alone meditate or write affirmations; it was all just too painful. I knew I had to try to write down something, get some of this out, but every time I did I would break down and cry again. I wanted to stay focused so I could help Frosty, but the truth is I was losing it. I didn't want to lose it, but I was. I assumed Frosty too was in agony, that he was in pain and in a strange place. I fought the urge to call the vet and say, "Give him back. I changed my mind. Just give him back." I finally was able to convince myself to pick up pen and paper and write a letter to tell God how I was feeling and beg him to make Frosty well. I wrote that if he was going to take Frosty to take him while he was at home. I know I wasn't making any sense and that I was trying to bargain with God, but I couldn't think of anything else to do. God, it seemed, had not heard me up to this point, so trying a letter would make it more real, and maybe, just maybe, this time he would hear me.

> *Dear God,*
>
> *I've been praying to you and praying to you and it doesn't seem like you are there or that you are hearing me. I am willing to believe that you are there and that you do hear my prayers and that all I have to do is ask and tell you what I can handle and what I can't. I can't handle this God, I just can't. I'm not strong enough.*
>
> *Debi made it sound so matter of fact when she said, "You told God you couldn't handle this and he will take care of it. Leave it to him." God, it doesn't feel taken care of. Frosty's suffering (at least I think he is). I can't stand that. There has to be another way to do this. God, can you hear me or are you even listening? Or maybe I have done something so wrong that you don't care to listen to me anymore. I don't understand all this and, well, I don't even know what to say to change it. I don't know anything anymore except that I can't do this, so I write you this prayer through a letter and I tell you again that I can't do this. Whatever plan or whatever lesson was set up in the past, before I came here to learn, I take it back. I can't learn it like this. It is too much. I take it all back. I don't know what I*

was thinking, but I take it back and I change it, recreate it, and I cancel all this pain and agony for Frizzy and for me. I just can't do it. Whatever I choose to give up close to me through all this pain I cancel now, and I create a new plan that involves love, gentleness, and good health. It isn't right to have Frosty suffer because of something I did or didn't do.

God, I know I sound negative, untrusting, and scared, but it's because I am. I'm willing to trust you, as long as you are healing Frosty now. That's the only way I can trust you.

I know you exist, I know there's a God, but years ago some things happened and I figured you didn't care about me anymore because you didn't make things okay then. You took those people away through very violent, painful circumstances. You want me to trust you, but how can I trust you if you let Frosty suffer and die? I stopped believing in you caring for me years ago. Maybe I stopped believing in you, maybe I was numb or mad, I don't know. But restore my belief in you. Show me you care and that you exist. Tell Frosty I am here, that I am with him, that I do love him. Tell him I am right outside the door, praying for him.

I believe, God, that you have the ability to create miracles, and I ask you to do that now, for him and for me. Cancel whatever was set up in the past and create a loving miracle. Yes, I know I can't make bargains with God and I can't play God and that is probably what I'm doing, but what I think I'm doing is telling you I can't do this, that I'm hanging on the edge of losing my faith, losing all hope that there is a God. I've read that you don't give more to people than they can handle. Well ... I can't handle this. I've lost too much in my life already, so much in my life has been related to death. Show me life, show me love, and show me miracles. I believe you can show me that and I ask for that now, a miracle for Frosty. I ask you to please return him to me in perfect health now.

Thanks for listening.

I knew I was begging and trying to make bargains with God, but I didn't care anymore. I just wanted this over. I just wanted Frosty back, healthy and feeling good, and I just wanted us driving to San Diego. I was fighting between believing and not believing, being mad and sobbing uncontrollably. I was at my wits' end. I was losing it. I wanted to hold him, to touch him. I wanted him well and happy again. I couldn't do this. I had to go get him, be with him, take care of him. I wanted to be the one to do that, not the people at the vet's office.

❧ CHAPTER 15 ❧

On Wednesday morning, I couldn't wait until the vet's office opened. I called one minute after they did. The vet said there wasn't much change, but it was hard to tell at this point. Frosty hadn't yet been on the IV for twenty-four hours, so he said it was just going to take more time. Oh, God, give me something to hold on to, anything. *Lie to me.* I fought the urge to call back an hour later, playing tug-of-war in my mind: should I go get Frosty or should I let him stay? Back and forth my mind went; it was exhausting. It took energy away from being able to send Frosty love and healing. I was wearing myself out. I kept praying for a direct answer on what to do, but I never heard it with all the screaming going on in my head. The answer probably did come, but I fought hearing it. I didn't want to hear it. There was only one answer I was open to hearing, everything else be damned.

I sat in the parking lot most of Wednesday, frozen, unable to leave, to write, or to do anything but think of Frosty. I truly was shutting down, going numb, and shutting out the world too. The few people who knew Frosty was back in called, but I only answered the phone once or twice. The others sent texts telling me it wasn't his time. I clung to those texts, telling myself they were right, that God had heard my prayers. They told me to keep busy, which would help keep me sane, and doing nothing was harder. I knew they were right, but I didn't want to leave Frizz. Leaving him was harder.

On Thursday morning I decided to go ahead and paint the wall in the workout room. I had bought the paint weeks ago, as I was scheduled to begin training clients again. I had forgotten about the air-duct cleaning that had been scheduled a few months ago. The man showed up with equipment in tow. I tried to be nice, but I wanted him to leave. I wanted to be alone, plus it meant I couldn't sit in the parking lot with Frizz. He said it would take about three hours. *Okay, think of it as a distraction and the paint smell will be gone by the time Frosty comes home.* I called the vet one more time before I started painting and spoke to one of the technicians. She went and checked on Frizz and said he responded when she called his name and was doing well.

I put on the *Instant Mood Brightner* CD and slowly started painting. It took about an hour and I started feeling better, counting on Frosty being home soon and me spending every minute with him. Everything really was going to be okay, so why couldn't I breathe?

Around one, I called the vet's office again. Yes, I'm sure they were tired of hearing from me, but when someone

FROSTY MY SPIRIT GUIDE

you love is in the hospital, you're there. I couldn't be there; calling was the only means I had to know how Frizz was doing. This time I talked to the vet himself. He said there had been no improvement. It took the wind out of my sails. I'd been going along the last hour thinking Frosty was better and there really was hope. This back and forth just made things harder. Hearing that just dropped me to my core. I hit rock bottom again and just didn't want to hold it together any more. I decided I would do better sitting in the parking lot of the vet's office—at least I would be closer to Frizz. Besides, painting seemed so insane to me. I booted out the air-duct man and once in the parking lot I felt better. I was closer to Frosty.

I sat there thinking about my decision and the tormenting thoughts about having him be there again. It was torture going back and forth: was it right or wrong, was it good or bad, were we going to have more time or had I wasted time? I was driving myself crazy. I ran a couple of errands trying to figure out what I wanted to do. I was leaning toward going to get him and just bringing him home because there had been no change in almost two days. Of course if I had stopped and faced myself in the mirror, looked myself in the eye and asked the question that I thought was too painful to ask, I would have known, but I was avoiding *me*. I had avoided my own eye contact, being too afraid to see. I had been avoiding Frosty's eye contact as well. I was avoiding looking, but now, well, now was different. I would give it one more night and if there was no change, I was bringing him home. I had felt so peaceful and right about having Frosty go back in, but I wasn't feeling that peace now. Just confusion.

While I sat in the parking lot that night, I rechecked Frosty's energy points in his body. I'd been checking them four or five times a day while he was in the hospital. As I checked them, it was the first time I was seeing that they were all in alignment. I was wondering how that could be. Maybe he was getting better. I checked them again just to be sure, and, yes, they were all in alignment. I panicked. How could they all be? Usually when someone is sick he or she is out of alignment and his always had been before now. I thought, *Someone who's close to being in spirit has perfect alignment of the energy in their body. Does that mean he is well, or that he is about to release his body and transition into spirit?* It was a thought I wiped clean before it could sink too deep. I wiped it away fast, but not fast enough. Something in me was beginning to give way to the truth, to what was really happening. I pushed it down, but a piece of it remained.

∽ CHAPTER 16 ∾

This night in the parking lot was only harder than the night before. This time, I felt as though I had nothing in the way of hope to hold onto. When I finally did go home, I pulled in the driveway and went to the back of the van to sleep there. I just couldn't make myself go into the empty bedroom one more time.

On Friday morning I climbed out of the van and headed into the bedroom to do a quick meditation before the vet's office opened. The bedroom was still dark. I turned on a small light in the room and turned to the bed. It took my breath away seeing the stuffed look-a-like of Frizzy sitting on the bed. It was a dog that looked like Frizz and was about the same size. I had been out shopping with a girlfriend about eight or nine months ago when she found the dog and said, "It looks like Frizz. You should get it." At the time, I hadn't thought anything of it, but I bought it anyway. I pulled out my timer and my candles for the meditation and, as I lit the candle, it seemed weird even for me, but the eyes on the stuffed dog seem to light up. Without thinking, I said, "You see the light, don't you?" I should have gotten that one, but I didn't. Well, maybe for a split second, but again my fear and not wanting to see blocked the reality.

The guilt comes in again now as I write because I should have known. Why didn't I know? I had continually allowed my fear to block what my heart kept trying to tell me. My fear was blocking communication with God and Frizz. I didn't get it and, yes, I still kick myself. This would all have been different for Frosty if I had chosen love over fear. I was in a hurry; I wanted to get to the vet's office. I wanted to bring him home. I didn't stop, and I didn't listen to my gut. Yes, I have guilt, simple as that. I have guilt.

I rushed through getting dressed, telling myself to hurry, hurry, hurry before it was too late. The last few days I had been feeling the clock ticking like I was in a race against time. I called the vet's office, letting them know I was coming over and a heads-up that I was considering bringing Frosty home that day. The vet wanted me to wait. I said we could talk about it when I got there. I could have stopped, but instead I picked up speed racing around so I could get there. *Hurry,* just kept screaming at me.

When I got to the vet, I was thinking it was time to bring Frosty home. If he wasn't any better then I would take him home. If he was better, that would be God's way of telling me to leave him another day.

The vet took me into a private room and pulled up Frosty's X-rays from that morning. He said again that it really didn't look all that bad, with just a small spot showing on the X-rays. He said the internist had examined Frosty and had not really found anything. He stressed again how important the IV was. He said that even though they didn't want to feed him, they offered him food just to see if he would take it and he wouldn't. I asked if I could bring him some from home and he said yes. I headed to the door to go home to get food for Frizz, then went back and asked one of the girls if they would use my phone to take a picture of Frosty. It was a way of me seeing how he was doing rather than actually going in and getting him all worked up. Going in during his last stay had shown me it was too stressful to have me come and go.

The girl came back with my cell phone and showed me the picture and asked if it was okay. I took a quick glance at it and said yes as I was walking out the door.

When I got outside, I looked at the picture. It was hard to look at it because it seemed like the lights were on inside Frosty, but no one was home. I saw it for a brief second, that gray color I had seen in people and animals that are about to leave their body.

My phone rang and I flipped it over and said hello. It was my girlfriend Shelley and her husband Dwayne, calling to check on Frizz. I talked while I drove. I went to the place I had been getting the fresh turkey breast for Frosty before he went in the hospital and picked some up. I headed back to the house to warm it up, all the while I was on the phone filling them in and trying to decide what to do about bringing Frosty home. I filled them in, telling them I would text them the new picture to see what they thought, but I mentioned that I was thinking if he didn't eat the turkey I was bringing him home today and that if he did eat it, I would let him stay one more day on the IV. I just wasn't sure that the treatment was working. I never considered that God had a different plan or that it might differ from my plan. I just always planned to be with Frosty when he transitioned.

I hung up the phone as I was walking back into the vet's office with the still warm turkey, telling them I would call later.

Upon walking into the vet's office, I started praying that Frosty would eat the turkey. I was scared he wouldn't because that would tell me what I didn't want to hear. The technician came up and I handed her the turkey. She unwrapped it and headed back to feed it to Frizz. She stopped at the door and turned around and said, "Do you want to feed it to him?" I said I would love to, but the doctor said it would upset Frosty to see me and then have me leave so I better not. Truthfully, I was afraid of seeing what I might see, but if I had only known what I know now, well, it's something I will regret for a very long time.

The tech headed back to Frosty and I sat down and held my breath. I heard her say to Frosty, "Look what your mama brought you." It was hard being so close and not being able to go to him. I prayed he would know it was from me. I kept thinking I wanted to be the one to feed him. I wanted to be holding the bowl for him, touching him, talking to him. I wanted to see him. I had to fight myself to not get up and walk back to him. I just wanted to see him, to know how he was. I prayed he would know I was right outside the door, that I loved him, and that I wanted him and that I wanted him home.

It took only a couple of minutes before the tech came back out with an empty dish. Frosty had eaten all the turkey that I had brought! I had brought enough, I thought, for a couple of snacks, as they weren't really feeding him while on the IV, but he had eaten it all. The tech and I hugged and everyone in the front office was cheering and I was laughing, crying, and smiling from ear to ear. Frosty was going to be okay, he was going to pull through this, and he would come home tomorrow! My fear was putting all those negative thoughts in my head. Frosty really was going to be okay. Tomorrow I told the tech, I'm taking him home.

I walked out carrying the now empty dish, but, as the door shut, it seemed like all the joy I had just been feeling faded away—as the door shut, so did a part of my heart. What was wrong with me? Why was my happiness so short lived? I was going to see him tomorrow, bring him home, hug him, spend more time with him, and he would be on his way to good health. Why was I holding back? My beloved, sweet Frizz, who had guided me through so many things, who had taught me so much, was coming home. This time tomorrow he would be home and I would be hugging him, telling him how much he was loved. Why was I holding back? Why wasn't I willing to stick with the celebration? I chastised myself for not being more open to the good. What was wrong with me?

On Friday night I slept in the van as usual, barely sleeping, wanting to be awake to count the minutes until I would see Frosty and really know how he was doing. I understood what the vet was saying about how important it was to have him be on the IV as long as possible, but I wasn't convinced that it was working, or was I just being selfish in wanting Frosty home? I didn't know any more. I really wanted to take him home. However, the vet wanted him to stay until Monday. If I was serious about picking him up, he suggested to let him stay so he could be on the IV until three o'clock. I was thinking noon or one at the very latest. I wanted him home. The back and forth in my head went on throughout the night.

On Saturday morning I got up and started preparing things for Frosty, so everything would be ready to bring him home. I would have nothing to do but be with him. I called the vet at a little past eight. He was tied up and I would have to call back. I couldn't stand this. I forced myself to start some long overdue laundry and clean up the house to stay busy, waiting for the vet to call back. I kept asking myself what was I supposed to be learning from all this, what was I missing? Louise Hay always said once you got the lesson, things would change.

It was about ten before I got to talk to the vet. He said Frosty was no better and he wanted him to stay throughout the weekend. I said no, if he was going to transition I didn't want him there alone. He said it was time to schedule a CAT scan of his stomach and he gave me the name of a place. I called and made an appointment for Monday as there was no one who could do it that day. I called the vet back to let him know. He again said it would be good to let Frosty be on the IV throughout the weekend. *No, no,* my head was screaming. I told the vet I wasn't okay with that and I would be over in a little while. I just couldn't bear the thought that Frosty might transition into spirit over the weekend. No, I couldn't leave him anymore. It was time to bring him home.

I jumped into the shower with that little voice screaming, *Hurry, hurry, hurry.* While in the shower I thought about what I needed to do, what I should do and how hard it really is to trust God's plan. I had always said I didn't want to be the one to make the decision of when Frosty would go. I wanted it to be by God's hands. I wanted desperately for Frosty to be okay, to feel good again.

I was in the shower when I finally came to a place of being ready to trust God and surrendering to his plan. I heard the thought go through my head and get stronger. I was ready to surrender to his will, to do the best I could with his plan, and it was then that I heard Louise again say that when you get the lesson, the person changes or the person leaves your life. It was then that I knew. God was going to take Frizz now, today.

I knew there wasn't much time. I quickly got out of the shower and began throwing clothes on. I just wanted to get there in time. I had come to a place of acceptance and in that acceptance I knew he was going to leave today. *Just let me get to him in time, please, please, God. Just let me be with him. Even if I couldn't get him home, just let me be with him. Oh God. Hurry, hurry,* I kept telling myself.

I was almost dressed when I felt something pass through me. It calmed me down a little. I wasn't sure what to think: was it God or Frosty telling me I had more time? I didn't know. It felt like peace with a thud. The phone rang and I jumped up to get it. It was the vet calling. He said Frosty was not doing well, I said I would be right there. It became a silent pray: *Hold on, hold on, please just hold on.*

Running to the car, I felt as though Frosty was already gone, that his spirit had already left his body. We put so much importance on the body, but it's the heart that carries the weight of the soul. Still, I wanted to be with him, to be there for him.

∾ CHAPTER 17 ∾

The rest you know. Frosty's physical body transitioned into spirit just seconds before I walked in. The shock, thankfully, set in immediately. His soul had passed through me when I was back at the house. The grief was overwhelming, making it hard to think. What was it Frosty was trying to tell me? I needed to know, but I would have to wait until later. First, I was desperate to get Frosty out of there and get him home.

I did take Frosty home with me that day, and on the way home, we went to the park just as I had promised him we would. No, it wasn't the same, but nonetheless we were together. There was pain and there was peace, but I also felt a numbness that I couldn't explain. I was grateful he was free of pain and I was grateful to have that time with him. I got to hold him and just be with him. It was a time much needed by my human self, because with Frosty being gone and the carpets being shampooed it was important to have him back in the bedroom. Having his physical body there in the room we had spent the most time in helped me to accept that he was now in spirit.

Frosty and I shared so much together for so long, so I wanted that time alone with him. It was something for me that had to be private, so I called no one. It was just too painful to think about, much less say. Everyone would know soon enough anyway. I couldn't cope with what other people would say or how they would or would not react. I didn't know how to react. I wanted to freeze up and stay numb, but I knew soon enough Frosty's physical body would be gone and I would have to deal with that transition as well.

∾ CHAPTER 18 ∾

*F*rosty's funeral came and along with it came the fear and panic of having to release his physical body. That scared me. I knew I couldn't hold onto his body forever, and I didn't want to, for his sake, but it was an enormous thing to adjust to. I didn't know if I could really handle it, but of course I was going to have to. I forced myself to think like a psychic, knowing I could still talk with him even after his physical body was no longer with me. I knew there were times when loved ones came to their families soon after their transition, others it took a little longer. I knew being numb would help, and forgiveness and love would keep me open to Frosty. I intended to do whatever it took.

I pushed myself to get ready and focused on spending the day taking care of Frosty's physical body. Once dressed, I reached for my rose quartz necklace that Frosty had been wearing before going into the hospital. I picked the necklace up by its chain and grabbed the rose quartz in my hand.

Immediately the thought came, *four days*. Four days popped into my head so clearly, as if someone had said it to me. Four days? What did four days mean? At first I was confused, and then I realized what it meant. I had taken the rose quartz off Frosty at the vet on Tuesday when he went into the hospital, and four days later he transitioned into spirit. I realized I'd have known that earlier if I'd held the rose quartz sooner. The crystal had told me, but I was too panicked at the time. Oh God, if I had stopped to listen. *If only, what if,* and then more *if onlys* were now setting in. No, I couldn't do this to Frosty. This was his day, his time. Today was about my sweet Frizzy. I would have plenty of time later to kick myself. Today was to be for him, which meant it was to be about love.

Getting the message from the rose quartz woke me up to the fact that I hadn't yet really felt Frosty's spirit as strongly as I thought I would. I know sometimes it takes time, but it seemed like I was on the verge of feeling him but then the feelings would stop. I wasn't afraid but curious, so, before we left the house, I knelt in prayer to ask. The answer came before I got up from my knees. My fear of actually seeing him in spirit would make it real for me and final, too real, and I was afraid not of seeing a spirit but of seeing him in spirit. I had not yet released his physical body and I was holding on to wanting him back the way he was in physical form. I wanted what we had. I had shut down to seeing him in spirit. I knew I would have to change that or risk creating a block between us. That was not a choice I was willing to settle for.

The cemetery had made special arrangements for Frosty, working in a private service. He was treated with great respect and love.

I was able to be with Frosty the whole time; he went from my arms to the arms of a man who had been taking care of the animals for over forty years. He seemed like an angel and I was left wondering, *Is he real or is he an angel?* He was angelic in his care for Frosty and the other animals he worked with. I will always be grateful for all the special arrangements and allowances that were made that day, knowing my best friend was being cared for with gentleness and love. The pain of course was there and beginning to build from the minute I released him, thinking that I would no longer be able to touch him or hug him. That thought increased my pain and my fear, so, while I waited, I picked up my paper and pen. Writing was something I had done for years and I knew writing to Frosty now would open a new door of connection for us. Yes, it was a different one, but a connection just the same.

When I was done writing, I sat there thinking about all that Frosty had brought to me and to my life. The letter had helped to bring about an opening, just as I thought it would. I had started the letter in grief, guilt, apologies of course, and concern for whether I was doing the right thing or the wrong thing with his physical body. I wondered desperately if he knew my love for him was there, even when his physical body was sick and ailing, that I had still wanted to take care of him, to be with him. I wrote about my anguish over this day and wanting to believe it would never come. I wrote that I was wondering and asking what Frosty was thinking and feeling about the day.

I wrote how I felt gratitude for him feeling now so comfortable with the newfound strength in his legs and that the pain was gone. I felt his joy and happiness overtake me and I felt his lightness, and the feeling of love was euphoric! What had started out as a letter of pain and unloading had become a connection of *divine* love. It brought me awareness, an opening into how Frosty and all our loved ones feel when they transition. Writing the letter gave me a knowingness that he was better than okay and that I too could and would be okay. I felt all the light, love, and goodness that he now carried. Our communication was clear and I was easily able to hear Frosty as if he was right there with me, and I knew that he was.

Writing so many letters throughout the years was my way of opening up communication through the mind—using my heart to hear. With Frosty, I didn't need to write to him because our communication had always been through the heart of our soul. Writing helped me to process my feelings by putting them down on paper. My grief subsided temporarily and I thought of how Frosty and all animals don't need us to talk at all. In fact, they prefer that we don't, at least not through our mouths. That is one of the many gifts those souls in animal bodies bring to us: the gift of silence. To hear them, we have to get quiet.

It's through Frosty that I was forced to practice communication from my spirit, which meant getting quiet.

If you have ever talked with a dog, a cat, a bird, a horse, or any type of animal, it is a very spiritual, humbling, from-the-heart experience. Thinking about that as I wrote my letter to him brought to mind how wise animals must be to teach us all that. How do they know to do that? Where does all that come from? How did Frosty know? I believe it comes from God. Maybe animals are more advanced than we think they are. It has been said by many, especially the animal experts, that we are all the same, that people and animals are all the same. We are all living things, furry body or body with skin. Animals breathe in the same way and just as much as we do. They are living beings. I realized my thoughts were running deep, but thinking about these things was bringing me more peace and helping me to feel Frosty. I was realizing just how much Frosty and all animals bring to our lives. There are some of us, me included, who learn better when the teaching comes from a soul in a furry body. God knows who the best teacher is for each one of us, and Frosty was the best for me. There has always been something in me that connected easily to animals and for most of us there is just something that allows for an opening in our hearts and a willingness to learn from the souls that are here in furry bodies. I was open to Frosty guiding me, which allowed me a connectedness that I might not ever feel or get to otherwise.

Frosty was continually leading me to God without me even realizing what he was doing. I just willingly followed, because I love him so much. Writing to Frosty now, he was still teaching me, leading me deeper into my soul, having to look at things I never imagined I could do at a time like this. I was writing to him, yet he was leading me in a place of peace. He transitioned such a short time ago and without any words spoken between us, he was still leading me to a place of peace and love. He was taking me with him into God's world, to the place of higher awareness.

It seemed as if I'd been writing forever, but it had only been twenty minutes. The funeral director said it would be about an hour and that she would come and get me. I looked down at the pages before me. I had intended to write Frosty a letter, but it looked as if he had written me one. I sat quiet for a minute, holding my pen in my hand and not knowing what else to write. It felt like there were no words. I couldn't help but think there was something to say. I thought of the hours that Frosty and all animals sit quietly, just listening, like they are in meditation. It sounds funny, but I realized, sitting in the parking lot of the cemetery, that not once did I ever hear Frosty say, "Hey, can you turn the TV on?" or "How about if we run to the mall to shop?" or "Can I barrow your cell phone so I can send out a text?"

Animals, well, they just listen. Their communication is all done through the heart, always with a quiet gentleness and the deepest of love, God's love, a love that we can only hope to attain in this lifetime. I was surprised to be sitting there in that moment feeling so calm. How could I be where I was and not be screaming for the men in little white coats to come get me? I was sure it was Frosty again, and of course God, covering me in a blanket of comfort, and for the moment I was accepting the comfort. I thought about how much comfort there was now in this place I was getting from Frosty, and it made me think of what a gift God has given us in all those souls in furry bodies. How amazing it is that dogs are leading the blind, assisting in drug busts, and sniffing out not only drugs but the criminals and other souls who have transitioned and released their bodies. They are the ones nudging us to know when a seizure is coming on or a diabetic black out is about to happen, and in my case it was Frosty telling me to call 911. It was he who would know before me that a family member needed help. It's our furry friends that are telling the deaf that their phones are ringing or that there's someone at their door. There are now furry friends who actually work underwater in search of our missing loved ones, and it's our furry friends that are in a lot of cases leading us and we are following them because we trust them, because God knew we would trust them.

Could it be that the souls we call animals are really messengers of God? I know that may sound dramatic to some people, but here I was, actually doing okay for the moment, and it was because of Frosty's love that I was feeling the peace, his peace, the peace he was sending me. He was leading me by example, and I was taking it from him just like I always had. It was like God's comfort and love were coming through my sweet Frizz. It was his transition day and he was comforting me.

Realizing that left me wondering whether to laugh or cry. It was like God himself was in Frosty's body guiding me to a place of peace. I remembered hearing a story of a man who prayed to God and asked if God would come to his home and have a meal with him. God said yes, so, on the appointed day, the man cooked up a big feast, invited family and friends, and they all got together awaiting the arrival of God. While they were waiting for God to arrive, a dog showed up and started eating all the food, just really eating it and enjoying it as a dog does. The man beat the dog off with a stick, yelling at him to go away. The dog ran off and the man, his family, and his friends continued to wait for God to come. As everyone left, the man dropped to his knees in prayer, asking God why he didn't come like he said he would. God replied, "I did come but you yelled at me, beating me off with a stick." The man, not understanding, said, "I never saw you." God said, "I wanted to really enjoy the meal you had prepared for me, so I came as a dog." The man was stunned, as most of us would have been. God is where he needs to be, when he needs to be, to help us learn what we came here to learn. Each of us learns in different ways and by different means, and there are those of us who learn what we need to learn through and by an animal's love, which is the same as God's love.

Animals come into this world with the ability to put love first and foremost above all else. They come into this world with the gift of awareness that they never lose. They reserve passing judgment and they forgive and love unconditionally. It seems like what we are all here to learn, the animals already know, so who is teaching who? That question brought to mind the time my oldest son, who has a gift with animals, attempted to train Frosty. He was good at it and was able to teach him to do certain things, but I always wondered who really was doing the training. Were we, the people, really training our furry friends, or were they training us?

Thinking about all this brought a fresh batch of tears to the surface. How was I going to do this without Frosty here in body, helping me, guiding me? Now what? This was never supposed to happen; this day was never supposed to come.

I was just signing my name on Frosty's letter when the funeral director motioned to me that they were ready for me, but was I ready for them? The grief surfaced again, threatening to overtake me and suck me under. It reminded me of labor pains: one minute I felt calm and was thinking maybe I could survive this. The next minute I wanted to start screaming in agony. But not now, now was for Frosty.

❧ CHAPTER 19 ❧

*W*alking mechanically to the van, my mind was racing and my body felt stiff. I was numb, thank goodness. That voice in my head was screaming, *How did it come to this? How did we get here? Oh God, how did we get here? It wasn't supposed to be like this.*

Now what was I supposed to do? I wanted to sit there frozen, waiting for God to take me, and at that moment he couldn't take me fast enough. There were other people coming into the funeral hall crying, and that was increasing the grief I was feeling. I knew I would have to leave. Had I done the right thing with Frosty's physical body? I wanted to be numb, to stop feeling the grief, the guilt, and this overwhelming panic that was stuck in my heart. He was coming back right, this was just a small, tiny illusion that was going to go away. He wasn't really gone, right? God, how long was this going to go on? I'm ready, God. You can bring him back now.

I looked around the van. What did I have left of him? None of this seemed right. This wasn't supposed to happen. It just couldn't possibly be. No, I wasn't going to accept this. God was going to bring him back. My heart was talking gently to me, but my mind just kept screaming—again the fear was there. This loss was just too great. I just couldn't do this. *Bring him back God, just bring him back. It was a joke right?* Where were all the signs that I pointed out to families and clients I had worked with, all those signs that your loved ones are there, that they *are* with you? Where were the blinking lights, the phones making weird ringing sounds or shutting off, the radio playing songs that would speak for them, saying, "I'm here"? Where were those signs? Just show me one, just one sign.

I wanted to let the panic take over, just let go and go crazy. This was way too mind-blowing. I was on the other side of the fence now. I had been working with families who had gone through the transition of a loved one and I always felt their loss and their pain, but this was intense. I wanted back on the other side. This wasn't supposed to happen; this day was never supposed to come. Well, I knew someday it would, but not today, not now. I hadn't even planned for it. Well, actually I guess I had in some ways, but I hadn't allowed my heart or my mind to prepare. I had prepared physically for the physical things, but how could I really prepare, how could anyone? How can I or anyone know what it was going to feel like before it actually happened? We couldn't know, even being there with other people, walking through it with them. It just wasn't the same. I was always feeling it through someone else's eyes. Well, not always. I had been through this myself before, but this felt so different.

Frosty and I had spent every day together for so long. I realized no matter how much I wanted to know and understand what someone else was going through, I couldn't. We feel it through our own eyes, because we can really only feel it through our own eyes. I was feeling that overwhelming panic coming on again. *Where are you, God?* I needed to calm down, I needed to feel Frosty, know he was there. What is it all the great teachers say? I took a breath, trying to calm down and clear my head. Oh, yes, I remember. Love the challenges that hurt you the most, be grateful for them, and that gratitude and love will transform the pain into acceptance and love. Okay, I had done that before, but right now it sounded insane. How could I love this? I didn't even want to try, but I had to for Frizz. Okay, I could sit here and say I love this. Pretend I love this and Frizzy would come back, right? I knew this could be a lot harder. People have been through more than this, not to minimize what I was going through in that moment, because this was really hard for me, but I knew people suffered bigger losses than this.

There I was again using that word: loss. I took a breath and pulled myself together. I took another breath. Okay, I would do this. Was I bargaining with God again? I was thinking I probably was trying also to control the outcome. Damn, maybe I couldn't do this. Maybe it would be better to just go insane. The thought popped in: just fake it till you make it. It was something Sonia Choquette always said, but it sounded like Frosty's voice. Okay, I would try that as long as it brought Frosty back. I told myself I was feeling calmer. I was feeling calmer actually. I tried to breathe and clear my mind. That's it. I could just lie to myself. I could fake it until I made it, just pretending I felt calm. The funny thing was that I actually did feel calmer, and I was beginning to feel something else, too—something familiar, something that had always grounded me and given me peace. The feeling got bigger, and I felt it right in front of me, as if it was sitting in my lap. I could feel his eyes staring at me, looking into mine. Frosty was here; he was with me. Thank goodness for signs, thank goodness for Frosty, and thank goodness for gratitude and Sonia and Frosty and peace. I could do this; I would just have to practice what I had been preaching. It had happened very quickly, but it was happening. I felt lighter, happier, and surer that maybe I could do this. It didn't have to make me crazy. Maybe there was some good that was going to come out of this.

Not even remembering when I got in the van, I looked around at Frosty's things and realized that those things could bring me either pain or they could bring me joy. The joy would open me up to Frosty and what he was now trying to bring me. Of course there was going to be pain, but I could have the joy mixed in. I got up to put things away, still feeling Frosty with me. I put the letter I had written to him in my folder with the thought of putting a blue cover over it and saving it.

A thought passed briefly through my head, like someone pushing again—you know the kind of pushing that is so gentle that you don't know you're being pushed. It was a thought that said, *I'm still with you, I'm still here, and I want the world to know that those they love are still here too.* I smiled because I knew it was true. My sweet, precious spirit guide Frosty was with me, and he was saying to me, *"I'm still here."*

∾ CHAPTER 20 ∾

I was wondering how long I would be allowed to sit in the cemetery parking lot. If I stayed, would they notice? Time moves so fast and yet it doesn't seem like that as life goes by. Where did all this start? When did it start? Why does it seem like it was just yesterday that Frosty came to me?

It all began a little over sixteen years ago. One of my sons had a red golden retriever. Yes, really she was red, like an Irish setter, but she was a golden retriever. We named her Angelic Puffy Happy Hansen. We called her Angel or Angelie for short. My oldest son had a black golden retriever. His name was Bam Bam, yes, just Bam Bam. Why there wasn't more to his name, I don't remember. Bam Bam was eleven at the time so we assumed he was no longer interested, but as a preventative he was put into a run to separate the two of them while Angel was in heat.

Pulling into the driveway one day, two heads instead of one popped up through the front gate to say hello! Funny, because Bam Bam had been in the run earlier. A few weeks later, Angelic was lying on the floor and I was rubbing her stomach. It felt bigger, like she had suddenly put on weight. I flipped her over more and realized she really had put on weight. Oh gosh, a light-bulb moment and off to the vet the very next morning we went.

Of course you know the news! Angel was only a year and a half old at the time so she was a little young, he said, but we would keep a close eye on her. Just two weeks after the visit to the vet, and just barely past New Year's Day, she went into labor. Talk about a quick pregnancy! Angelie succeeded, despite her age, in delivering seven healthy puppies: one black, one gray, four gold, and one very white one—yep, guess who! We called him Frosty because we were still in the Christmas mode and he was white so Frosty the Snowman fit him perfectly. He was the first one to have his name and of course it stuck with him.

Now, I'm pretty sure a lot of you are thinking, *Oh, how cute and how fun! Seven cute little puppies to love and kiss.* Well, I got to tell you, it was! I was in heaven. We had set up a big box the size of a spa that angel could deliver her pups in and she did really well for as young as she was. In the mornings I washed sheets, towels, blankets, and tearing paper into strips by hand. The afternoons I spent hugging, holding, kissing, and of course tearing more paper. Getting an electric paper shredder gave me the same feeling as winning the lottery! As the puppies grew, so did their barks (and their poop), so they were moved into the garage as it was still too cold and rainy to put them outside. The door to the house was left open, so the heat could filter out and of course so the puppies could continue to be spoiled and so Angel could get to them. When the puppies were about four weeks old, two more spa boxes were added. The kids in the neighborhood started calling it the doggie condo and actually it did look a lot like a condo. The puppies could run in and out from one box to another, making it seem as though there were different rooms to their house. Two or three times a day the puppies would be taken out of their condo to run around in the garage. It was loads of fun chasing down seven puppies.

Angel was given supplements so she could keep feeding her litter, but it was obvious she was a little on the tired side. She enjoyed her short breaks in the yard without all the puppies hanging on her. When the weather was dry, the puppies got to play outside too, but not when Angel was having her private time. It was amazing to see how they would respond when they saw her, running to her as hard as they could. It was the food tray they saw in her. As each puppy started to grow into its own personality, it would be given a nickname. This made it easier to tell who was who. They would be renamed later on, of course, as their new families took them home.

They were all so very cute, with each one having their own special personalities. Keeping one puppy was only a thought as anyone who has dogs knows that two is a lot and three are, well, more than the normal person could handle. Frosty, surprisingly, was never the one considered for keeping. He was very cute and, being the only white one, he was a standout and people were always drawn to him. It was a given that he would be one of the first to go, when the time came, although he was a bit stand offish with most people, kind of snooty really. He didn't seem to care about interacting with the other pups or the people who came to check out their future furry friend. He was content to play on his own. He always seemed so confident and sure of himself. The other pups would try to play with him, but he really wasn't interested.

During outdoor time, Frosty could usually be found lying in the center of my flower garden. He loved them. The door would open and he would head straight for the flowers. But I understood, I was big into the flowers too.

Throughout his life, when I brought the weekly bunch of flowers home for the bedroom, he would stand waiting while I cut them so he could sniff them before I put them in the vase. I would have to stick them up to his noise so he could smell them before he was satisfied. He just loved flowers. He never chewed them up or dug them up. He would just lie in them and smell them.

He was also the only puppy to go for my shoes. The funny thing was that it was only my running shoes. He loved them. He never chewed on them but just tried to drag them around by their laces. At that time, the shoes were about the same size as Frosty. Looking back now I wonder, *Was he trying to tell me something? Could he have known then, what I know now?*

∾ CHAPTER 21 ∾

*S*o how was it that Frosty came to stay and be my spirit guide? Well, as I said before, I was born an animal person so I was thrilled with having seven puppies to care for. I really was having the time of my life, however I was learning as I went along. I had never raised puppies before, so I didn't know that it was important for the puppies to have their first shots before people came in to see them, especially if they were going to pick them up.

I noticed Frosty seemed a little calmer than usual. He typically was not one of the rowdier puppies, so at first it didn't stand out to anyone but me that there might be something wrong. Frosty and the other leader of the pack, we called him Speck because he had a speck on his forehead, were both very calm. Anyway, I asked if anyone else noticed Frosty being slow or not as playful as usual. No one noticed anything at first, so I chalked it up to him being around five weeks and he was just developing his personality. The next day we had the puppies out front and a neighbor came by, a neighbor who had taken a special interest in Frosty, so when he saw him out front, he picked him up and held him. The neighbor said, "I think there is something wrong with him. He seems kind of out of it." I took Frizzy to the vet. As it turns out, he had canine hepatitis. The vet said that humans can be a carrier from their dog to another dog. The risk is higher of course if the dogs are young and have not had their shots yet. I had no idea something like that could happen and lucky in the long run Frosty was fine, but for the moment it meant that he would have to be separated from his brothers and sisters. It meant that someone was going to have to feed him because he couldn't be fed by his mother with the other pups. He would have to sleep in a separate box. It didn't sound very fun for Frosty, but with all the attention he got, I don't think he minded very much.

Little did I know what the future would hold as a result of him getting sick, and at that time knowing whether he was strong enough to pull through was anybody's guess. What a divinely beautiful plan God had cooked up. Of course I couldn't see it at the time. All I saw was a puppy suffering and not feeling too good.

Someone I was very close to recently transitioned into spirit and I hadn't gotten over it yet. I'd been asking God to send someone to fill that gap. Now I know that no one can be replaced, but I was hurting and asking for the grief to heal, and at that time I thought someone else could heal it. I humorously had been asking God to send me someone who would want to be with me twenty-four hours a day. It's true what they say: be careful what you wish for. Frosty picked me long before I picked him or even realized he had picked me. When he became sick, I became his mama and he was so open to transferring his love that he must have known he was part of God's plan.

One of the big spa boxes was placed in my room at the foot of the bed and he began sleeping with me. I fed him by bottle and set the alarm clock at night to make sure he was still breathing and okay. At first he was pretty calm, since he wasn't feeling very well, but with all the one-on-one care he was getting, he was fast recovering to a state of mischievousness and play. It was great to see him getting stronger and back to his old self.

As he got stronger, I would take him outside to play. That period of time put a hitch in his social skills. He wasn't being socialized in a way that a puppy would normally be. He was being socialized by us humans who were taking care of him. He had his new mama and the family and that seemed to be all that he needed. He adjusted very well and seemed happy.

It took a couple of weeks, and he was almost ready to be put back with his brothers and sisters. He was still sleeping in the box, but one night toward the end of his isolation period, I was asleep and I felt this thud on the bed. Yes, of course, I was startled, thinking we were having an earthquake. I sat up rather quickly and flipped on my light and there, just

BETHANY-ELIZABETH FAYE HANSEN

as sweet as you please, was Frosty on the bed! I'm not sure what suddenly made him think that he could climb up, or of climbing up at all, but he was so pleased and happy with himself, it was like he was grinning from ear to ear to show me what he had done! I said, "Yahoo," and put him back in the box.

The next night, Frosty was more careful when he climbed up on the bed, so as not to wake his new mama up. It wasn't the thud that woke me up this time but the hot breath of a furry friend in my face! He was standing over me, as if to whisper, "See what I did!" I couldn't help but laugh.

You had to love him because his personality was so full of humor. The whole in-and-out-of-the-box thing became a great nighttime game for Frizz, and it continued for another three or four nights until one night, when I had put him back in the box and he couldn't manage to get back up on the bed, he whined and barked very softly. He started out being very quiet about it, until his patience wore down and then he got louder. I, of course, was under the covers trying not to let him knowing I was laughing. After all, I had to at least pretend to be in charge. I sat up once and said, "Frosty, no. Pipe down. It's night-night time." He stopped for a few minutes, long enough for me to escape to the bathroom to regain my composure and go back to pretending I was in charge. He was just so cute. When I came back from the bathroom, this is what was waiting for me.

Well how could I, or anyone, resist that? I lifted him up, put him on the bed, and he lay down, taking up an amazing amount of space for a small puppy. Lucky for me he did go back to sleep. I made a mental note to ask the vet in the morning, if Frosty was ready to be put back with his pack.

As it turned out, the vet said to wait a few more days before putting Frosty back. In those few days, Frosty realized he could now reverse the game. He could run flying off the bed to pounce into the box, and then he would make his low whine, softly of course, so as not to wake up his mama. Sometimes in the excitement of the game, the whines would turn to barks, very loud wake-up-the—whole-house barks.

It was during this time that Frosty found himself getting a little bored with Mama, as she didn't play as much as he wanted her to or as rough and wild as he needed. He went in search of something or someone wilder to play with. He had his stuffed toys that he carried around, but he treated them with love. He slept with them and kissed them, but he would never chew them up. They were his friends and they didn't wrestle back. He needed play toys that were bigger and rowdier than him so there would be a little competition. He found it in one of my sons who had the courage to throw himself on the ground in the middle of all the puppies.

Frosty wrestled with my son, with the rest of the pack before he got sick, so having my son lie on the floor now, was an open invitation for Frosty to attack him, in play of course. Since it was now just the two of them, Frosty played with my son like one of the other pups: biting at him, tugging on him, and barking at him. Frosty loved to climb over him! I don't know who was laughing harder, my son or Frosty. It was because of these wrestling matches that Frosty got his first nickname. We started calling him Bite-a-Kiss. We called him that because he would bite mainly on the nose, but anywhere else would work just as well. The bite was soft like a kiss, so it was as if he was kissing you with his teeth. He loved doing the bite-a-kiss thing with my son, and my son being the rowdy hurricane that he was, of course would bite back. Frosty would get so excited that he could hardly contain himself, and he would bark so loud that my son would have to cover his ears. Frosty had a new play toy and a way to wear out my son. It worked great and created so much fun for everyone!

At the end of Frosty's incubation period, it was finally safe for him to be put back with his brothers and sisters. We decided that installing a small run would give the puppies a change of scenery and make the transition of bringing Frosty back into the group easier on all of them.

That time of incubation had clearly put a hitch in Frosty's social skills with the other pups and with people. His doggie mother had not socialized him; he had been socialized by us humans. He didn't fight with the other pups, but he clearly had no need for them. He took on a more snooty personality than he seemed to have before he was sick. He had no need for other people because he had his new mama. Yes, I admit, he was been just the teeny, tiniest bit spoiled, but he'd been sick and needed the extra care.

By this time, I still hadn't considered keeping Frosty, but of course he had already decided he was keeping me—I didn't know that at the time. Now that he was well, as far as I was concerned, he too would be ready for a family, along with the rest of them. Five of the seven puppies had families waiting to take them home. It wasn't long before there were three families asking about the white one. He was stunning being so white, with his dark black nose and strong legs. His snootiness now came off as an air of confidence and wisdom and he walked with a surety the other pups didn't have. All of that made him very desirable.

I set about interviewing the three families interested in Frosty. They were all friends of friends, but my desire was to get the best match for everyone. I had the potential families come over so I could see how Frosty responded to them and how they responded to Frosty. The first two families were not going to work. Frosty was not giving them the time of day; he clearly wanted nothing to do with them. He was his normal snooty self. The third possibility was a single female about the same age as me, with the same eye and hair coloring and a similar body build. She came over and things went pretty well, and Frosty seemed more interested in interacting with her than he had with the other families. In fact, he did great. It never occurred to me that Frosty was fine with her, because it never occurred to him that this might be his new mama. The lady came over a few times. Each time they both seemed to accept each other and so I decided this could work out. I visited her home and we agreed Frosty would be hers; she just needed a week to have a fence put up. She called me four days later, telling me that she and her house were ready and she was very excited. It was decided I would bring Frosty to her at the end of her Kinko's shift and she would take him home from there. Heading over to Kinko's that day, I found it a little strange that I wasn't feeling nervous or sad. Maybe, just maybe, I was just going through the motions, never intending for Frosty to go anywhere. I don't know, but God had a plan.

I walked into Kinko's carrying Frosty, with my kids in tow. I placed Frizz up on the counter and his new mommy came over to us. She went to reach for him and he barked, just once. It startled all of us, but we all laughed at first. She hesitated, then reached out again as she was talking to him. He let out a growl. Literally, this twelve-week-old puppy growled at her. It was the type of growl that he was saying in no uncertain terms did he want anything to do with her. We all shared an uncomfortable moment, then we laughed nervously. She said, "I don't think this is going to work." I said, "I think you're right."

I picked up Frosty, we walked out and went *home*, and that was the end of that. No one ever mentioned anything about that or finding a home for Frosty ever again. He was home and he had known that all along.

∾ CHAPTER 22 ∾

*S*till sitting in the parking lot of the cemetery, my brain was screaming at me, *You can't sit here! You can't stay here! You have to move! You have to do something!* I was stuck in the past, wondering how all that time had gone by so fast.

I knew I couldn't stay in that parking lot forever, but I was frozen. Had I done the right thing? I started back into the questions. I knew if I sat there longer, it would get worse, and since God obviously wasn't going to take me now, I figured I better do something, but what? I felt so frozen and numb, which is a feeling I was becoming all too familiar with. Sitting there was going to make it worse. For Frosty's sake, I forced myself to start the van for the second time. I heard a voice in my head say, *Put on your How to Be Happy CD.* I pushed it in. I didn't want to, but I had promised Frosty I would. I knew being happy helps open me up to feeling him. I put my foot on the gas and pulled out of the cemetery parking lot. I was numb. I got about four blocks down the street and the grief and the panic started to set in again. Is this how it was going to be, a constant battle of my two wills? Why couldn't I celebrate for Frosty? I knew he was still here. I knew that without a doubt, yet this change was not working well for my human self. This back and forth between love and grief was exhausting. The *How to Be Happy* CD started skipping around in the player. It was, for a minute, a distraction from my grief. I pulled it out, considering chucking it out the window. I felt a rush of anger. *Okay God help me out here, you want me to listen to this, then make it work.* Wow. Where had that come from? I hadn't realized how angry I was.

I put it back in and it skipped again. I hit the eject button, wanting to punch it, but fought against it. I had to be in a place of love to feel Frosty. The CD popped out and the radio blared. It was a woman singing, "stuck like glue." It confused me for a minute. The light turned red. I stopped and sat there with the CD in my hand with the woman still singing. My brain was so foggy. What was bugging me about this song? I had never heard it before. She was back at the chorus, "stuck like glue." A small smile started across my face. I knew our loved ones reach out to us through music and I usually have a song going in my heart. The song ended, but by then I was laughing. The song was from Frizz! He was already sending me messages!

I got to the computer as soon as I could and Googled "stuck like glue" and up popped Sugarland's song, "Stuck Like Glue." I headed to the nearest store to pick up the CD.

On my way there, I received a text from Dwayne in Arizona. He at this point did not know Frosty had transitioned. He was just working through divine order. His text read, "Have you heard Sugarland's new song?" I laughed and thought, *Yes, Frosty, I have.* I found the CD, paid for it, headed out to the van, and popped it in. I listened to the words, which made me laugh, especially the first line, "Absolutely no one knows me better." And no one does. Thank you, Frizz!

∾ CHAPTER 23 ∾

The morning after Frosty's service, I woke up early, forgetting everything, and then I sat up and remembered. Maybe the nightmare was over and Frosty was here. I looked around. I felt him here. Everywhere I felt him, so close and yet so far.

One of my closet's friends, Debi, wanted to hang out today, shop, and go to lunch to celebrate my birthday. I didn't want to go. I didn't want to celebrate. I wanted Frosty. I wanted to go back. I had some things to finish up for Frizz and his day from yesterday and his transition. I wanted to do those things for him today. I was in a fog, not thinking, just putting one foot in front of the other. Some people call it autopilot, and I call it brain fog. I sat on the floor, not wanting to move. A text came in from another friend: "Frosty wants you to go play, he's happy when you're happy." I knew it was true, but my guilt wanted me to stay home. I wanted to stay home. My grief and my guilt said I should be home screaming, wailing, and crying. If I wasn't in a hole mourning this horrific loss, then Frosty would think I didn't love him. What kind of people go out celebrating when someone they love is dead? He would think I was glad he was gone. I couldn't go party when my best friend had just transitioned. I wanted him back. I wanted to mourn. I knew celebrating was something those who have transitioned into spirit did, something we to could do, but I wasn't there yet, not at that moment anyway. I wanted him back. Why, God, why did you do this? No, I had to be mourning so Frosty would know I miss him and that I still loved him.

Debi called to see what time I wanted to meet. She knew about Frizz and how hard this was for me. She gently coaxed me into going. She said, "Frosty would want you to." Gosh, he was working through all my friends. I know this is divine order. She had asked me about this day months ago. I had thought off and on about canceling because Frosty hadn't been feeling well and I wanted to spend my time with him. I hadn't canceled because somewhere inside I knew I should go. I let Debi talk me into meeting in the afternoon, but there were some things I wanted to do first.

I had only talked with a few people about Frosty's transition and there weren't that many more who had even known he was sick. I was going to need some help with some of this, so I asked God how to get done what I wanted to get done. Minutes later, I got a text from my girlfriend, Artemisa. She knew about Frosty and had known all along. She had been one of my major supports through this whole journey. She asked if I needed anything. I told her what I needed done and she dropped everything to meet up with me, which surprised me because that's not something she could normally do. I was very grateful, as she was very comfortable with loved ones transitioning. She and Frosty had always been kindred souls and the love and connection she has for animals has blessed her with the gift of hearing them and Frosty always spoke to her. It was divine order that she was the one there with me that day. Things just fell into place with such ease and I was feeling more peace knowing Frosty was by my side. I noticed, as I felt more joy, that Frosty became more active and it was easier to feel him around me. I felt lighter, happier even, which was strange. The guilt tried to push itself through, but I pushed back. I liked what I was feeling. Having someone with me, who was comfortable with the process, had made a big difference, and it helped me to see that letting people in wasn't as bad as I thought it would be.

We got done just as my other girlfriend, Debi called, letting me know she was in town and could meet whenever I was ready. I told her I could meet her at two p.m. I was feeling better, but still tired, but I knew it was a push from Frizz to go. So many times people work through us as a way of getting support to a loved one and we don't even know it.

Back in the van my cell phone rang. I hesitated to answer it. I was avoiding many people so I didn't have to tell them about Frosty. At some point, I knew I would have to, but when I was ready. I looked at the caller ID, it was one of my long-time girlfriends, who not only knew about Frizz, but she was one of his favorite people. I said hello and started to cry. That was okay with her. She loved him so much she just cried with me. It took us a couple of minutes of muddling through, and then I said, "So what's up? Why did you call?" She said she was just checking to see if I was going through with my birthday plans and how I was feeling. I said, "Yes, I'm going, even though I really don't want to. I feel like a limp noodle." She asked how my hair was, which was normal for her because she's also my hair dresser. I said, "dirty ponytail." She said, "Come by the salon right now and I'll do your hair. See you in a few. I'm waiting." She hung up, and I started to cry. She'd always been so supportive with me and Frosty. The way she worded it made me feel like I had to go.

I was surrounded by so much love and support. I was grateful, and yet in some ways it was so hard to take. I just wanted my sweet, precious Frizzy back. I knew it sounded like I wasn't grateful, but I was and I wanted to be, because I knew that gratitude would open me up to feeling and seeing Frosty.

I got my hair done and then headed over to meet Debi. I had everything Frosty had ever touched or played with in the van. It was quite a sight, but it made me feel better and I found myself laughing at it all. It was like he was there and had dragged it all out to the van himself. It was funny how I felt so up and down.

My cell phone rang and I felt myself tighten up again. I just didn't want to talk to people. It was too hard to pretend to be cheery. I hadn't been returning phone calls, texts, or e-mails, and I knew at some point my friends would become more forceful in wanting to know what was going on with me. I knew I couldn't keep avoiding or hiding forever and it was getting harder, not everyone in my immediate family had been told yet, but it was just too hard to hear myself say it out loud.

I decided not to answer. I would call back. Within minutes the phone rang again and a text came through. It was like a dam had burst and Frosty was saying, *I'm not going to leave you alone. Enough isolation. You deserve to live and to be happy.*

Debi and I did get together that day, sharing stories of our furry friends as well as family and friends who were now in spirit. We hung out long into the night with some moments being happy, some sad. The time we spent together helped to push me past the grief and into seeing how many people were really going out of their way to support me in this. I realized that there were people in my life who really did understand how hard this was for me. As a result of that day, I stopped telling myself that I shouldn't cry. I saw how releasing the grief actually made way for the joy, and it was in those moments of joy where I was open to feeling the most amount of love.

It was that same day that I began to see the importance of laughter. My family had never been much for laughing, and I saw how having a sense of humor can really help in the healing process. I hadn't felt much like laughing, as this was no laughing matter to me, but seeing that it opened the door even more to feeling Frizz and my other loved ones was all the encouragement I needed. I began the practice of laughing through my tears.

～ CHAPTER 24 ～

*T*he next day I was to meet up with another girlfriend, Melissa. It was her turn to "babysit" me—my words, not hers. She laughed when I told her. It felt like that because someone was calling me everyday to drag me out of the house, to make sure I wasn't alone. A part of me still wanted to be alone, at home with the covers pulled up over my head. I knew Frosty wanted me out and interacting. It was a way to help bring the joy in and today would be easy in the sense that Melissa believes the same way that I do: that Frosty is still here. It made it easier on me because I could tell her the things that I saw.

The day started off with another one of Frosty's gifts. I was on my way to meet her, fighting between the grief and the joy I was feeling from him. I pushed in the *Stuck Like Glue* CD that Frosty had sent me on Monday. "Stuck Like Glue" was the third song on the disc and I let it play through. I was a little early meeting Melissa, so I sat there listening to the first two songs; by then I had been sitting in the van for three to four minutes. The second song ended and "Stuck Like Glue" started up, and right away I felt this happy peace roll over me. I knew from past experience that Frosty was there. I could feel him. Words popped in my head—Sing, Mama, sing—so I started singing the words to the song. As I did, I noticed Frosty's choke chain that was now hanging on the rear-view mirror start to dance. It was an amazing sight! It gave me goose bumps and the hair on my arms stood up. It was the same as if he was right there! I was laughing and feeling so much joy! I wanted to stay in this place so I could be open to this all the time.

Frosty always rode in the back of the van on the couch where it was safer for him. But that day I felt him in the passenger seat. It was such a kick for both of us to have him up front! Getting that song was so perfect because music had always touched us both and had been something we both loved. It was a way of communicating, then and now. Frosty was a puppy when I first realized he loved music. He would walk over to the piano and gently smack his mouth on the keys to make it play. I almost changed his name to Beethoven because of it. He loved the guitar and he loved it when I sang. Music brings peace and it brings messages; it's a way our loved ones reach us. Music has always been an opening to my soul. I knew hearing a song over and over it was one of my loved ones in spirit talking to me, giving me a message. Now more than ever it was important for me to listen to it.

Melissa took me to dinner and then I played the song for her. After that, she insisted we go shopping. I was wondering if she, Debi, and Frosty were all working together on this. I hadn't been taking care of myself well. In recent years I had been busy with other family members, and more recently my focus had been on Frizz. Now my girlfriends were saying it was time and of course they were telling me Frosty wanted me to. We shopped for a few hours and it was there shopping with Melissa that I realized Frosty no longer had to wait in the van. Now he could go in and shop with me. It was something that takes getting used to. Spirits can go anywhere, yes, anywhere. Where are your loved ones following you?

Driving home that night was hard because I kept telling myself I was alone. I knew I wasn't, but the fear of being alone with my feelings was coming back again. The thought popped in that I could ask to be shown that I wasn't alone, so I asked—not really thinking about it but just asking. It was only a few minutes when I heard something in the back of the van. I wanted to look, but I was afraid to look. I pulled over and looked back and on the floor was one of Frosty's favorite toys. I was surprised because I always made sure things were put where they would stay. I could tell myself it had just fallen off in the ride, but I knew it hadn't. I felt Frosty there, I saw the flash of movement, and I felt his laughter just like when he would tease me. I got up and went to the back of the van, laughing. I said, "Frosty, you can't be doing this while I'm driving, but thanks for the sign." I felt better, but—and yes, there is a but—I knew what I knew, and I knew he was there. But this change thing is something

I wanted to resist. We humans don't like change. I couldn't hug him in the same way that I used to. I wanted what I wanted. This was different, so I was concluding that it was bad or not as good as before. Well, in some ways it was better. I was able to smile through my tears.

❧ CHAPTER 25 ❧

Today is my birthday, and it's also Thanksgiving Day. Now what? I refused to answer the phone or be around anyone. It was all too new; I just couldn't fake it today. There were cards and gifts sitting there to open, but no way was I going to do that. It hurt way too much. I showered and dressed and forced myself to put on the red sweater my girlfriend had given me for my birthday a few days earlier. *Fake it, just fake it,* I kept telling myself. I could maybe fake it as long as I was alone, being around people today was just too much. I decided I would spend some time at the cemetery where Faye's body was buried. I would take some flowers, which I still did, even though I knew she was with me. It would be peaceful there and the quiet would help me connect more.

I stopped and got flowers, and memories of when Frosty and I would come here came into my head. I never let him out on the grass. I was always afraid he might go to the bathroom on someone's headstone. He would stand at the van window and watch, with a toy hanging from his mouth, wagging his tail so hard the back end of his body went back and forth too. It always seemed to me as if he was saying, "I know her, let me out." Sometimes he would get so wound up, he would bark a funny bark because he was trying to bark through the toy clutched in his mouth. He would stay at the window, watching until I came back. This time I put off getting out, I didn't want to look back and see that empty window. I couldn't bear it. I sat for a while thinking about how fast your life can change.

I cut the flowers and headed to where Faye's physical body had been buried almost thirty years ago. Funny how I never thought of her being gone, because she was always here. It's been so long, yet I have known her longer in spirit than I did in her body. I knelt down, putting the flowers in the holder, and listened for what she had to say. The tears came and I asked her to help me through this and to help me keep Frosty close. I stayed for a few minutes, but, force of habit, I wanted to get back to Frosty. I walked back, praying for a sign that he was with me. I got back in the van to the sound of my phone ringing. I didn't want to talk with anyone, but I felt the push to look at the caller ID. It was my friend Artemisa, who had helped me with Frosty. I knew Frosty would continue to communicate with her, so I picked up the phone, not wanting to miss a chance to connect with him.

We talked about Frizz and what I was doing and where I was. During the course of the conversation, I moved back to my seat next to the couch where Frosty always sat. I was facing out the back window when I noticed a small SUV pull past me, swing around, make a U-turn to come back to park on the opposite side of the street, even with the van. An older man got out of the driver door and an older lady got out on the passenger side, another man in his thirties got out from the back drivers side. Normally, I would not have given all this a second glance, but something was drawing me to them, especially the younger of the two men. He went to the back of the SUV and flipped up the rear door and out jumped Frizzy! No, it wasn't my Frizz, just looked like him. My heart skipped a beat! My sweet, precious Frosty was showing himself to me. He was telling me, "I'm still here." The dog ran all over the grass on strong legs, flying like the wind. He had the energy of a puppy and appeared to be the picture of health. I knew it was Frosty's way of saying to me, "Look, I'm healthy, my legs are strong, and I am with you. I can run as fast as I want to now!" I was so excited. At first my girlfriend had a hard time figuring out what I was telling her. Once she figured it out, we were both laughing. I told her I would call her back, and, as I hopped out of the van, the furry ball of energy went flying by me. I didn't know whether to laugh or cry. The dog seemed so happy and filled with joy, another thing I was sure Frosty was trying to communicate to me. I walked toward the dog's owner and, as I started to speak, a sob came up, sticking in my throat and making it hard to talk. He said, "Is he bothering you?" I said "No, my golden just transitioned a few days ago."

That was all I could get out. Luckily he was a doggie lover and had been through it a few times himself. He talked about his furry friends that had been with him before their transitions and he talked about the one that was running around on the cemetery grounds. He said his furry friend was nine, which is the same age that Frosty seems to be to me when I see him in my mind's eye, since his transition. It was another validation that I was grateful for.

While we were talking, the ball of energy continued to run around, sniffing, and, yes, even peeing on the grass. Suddenly he realized the door to the van was open. The furry bundle of energy headed to make a flying leap, intending to land inside. The owner whistled and the furry friend stopped just short of the van door. I laughed, as my heart sang with a knowingness of what had just happened. What a great birthday present Frosty had given me, and what a great birthday it was turning out to be! I was amazed that I could go through Frosty's transition and have even a second of joy, but here I was actually smiling.

I stayed at the cemetery until dark, receiving a text just as I was heading out. The text read, "You should see the new Disney movie, *Tangled*. You'll love it!" It was from a friend who didn't know Frizz had transitioned. Someone else had mentioned that to me earlier in the week, and I had seen the commercial about it as well. I believe divine messages come to us in threes and that was three.

The thought occurred to me that I could go now. I was thinking, *What is the hurry?* Going to the movies was not my big thing, and going by myself is something I had never done before, but as I thought about it the push came again to go. I resisted. It was done in animation and I really was not into it. The push came again. I gave in thinking, *What the heck,* and next thing I knew I was sitting in the movie theater, waiting for the movie to start.

I sat there thinking how strange life is. I was feeling sad and happy at the same time. I was feeling something else too, but I didn't know what it was. It had been that way all day, something that I had felt before but not as intense. I realized the feeling was connected to when I was working and doing intuitive readings for people. It was what I call a light-bulb moment. The thing I was feeling was Frosty in spirit next to me—yes, next to me in the movie theater. Wow, that had never happened before. I was used to him waiting in the van. Maybe there were some positives to this.

The movie had lots of music in it, and for me music always touches my soul so I was sucked in right away. It had lots of funny moments and it was striking a cord in me. There was something familiar about most of the characters. The horse in a strange way reminded me of Frizz, so it lightened my heart even more. Toward the end of the movie, during one of the songs, the female character was singing, "It's like the fog has lifted." Something inside me shifted. It was like I was feeling love for the first time. How could that be? How could I be feeling so much love now? But I was, and as the movie ended with tears streaming down my face, I turned toward where I had seen Frosty sitting at the beginning of the movie. He was still sitting there. I looked at him through my tears of happiness and I realized it was like they sang in the movie: now that I see you, really see you, I'm not afraid.

It's true. Only love is real and in the midst of darkness and pain … Only love is real.

I knew I would want to see that movie again. There was so much in it, but for today I was ready to go home. And as I walked out of the theater, I felt and heard a messenger of God tromping next to me with his tail wagging and his head held high. He was here to teach me about love and he was doing just that.

Thank you, Frizz, and thank you, God.

∾ CHAPTER 26 ∾

*F*riday morning, I woke up feeling happy and down. I had really looked forward to spending Thanksgiving with Frizz. I woke up knowing it was time to sit with this, no running around and no turning to friends. Going within me was something I assumed would be painful, so I kept putting it off.

It wasn't as hard as I expected it to be. I did a lot of meditating and prayer and, by the end of the day, the idea for this book had been placed in my head. I'd been working on another book for the last two years. It had been slow going, but ok. I wasn't really big on the idea of starting another book now, especially when I felt so raw. But suddenly here it is: *write all this down.* I hadn't done any journaling since Frizz got sick, which was unusual for me. I was twelve when I started journaling. It was my escape, my way of processing, but now to even pick up my journal, I just couldn't do it. The thought of writing out everything, putting it on paper, no, I couldn't do it. I filed that in the back of my head. If it came back, I would think about it.

I needed to get outside. I knelt down in prayer, asking for Frosty to be with me today. I knew I would have to keep asking. As I headed out to the van, I heard that familiar tromp, tromp next to me. I smiled. It almost felt like old times, except now there were tears behind the smile. I was getting back in the van after the second errand, getting in by the back passenger door as I always had, jumping in with my usual "Hi Frizz," forgetting everything for just a minute. I had forgotten. I was on my way back to his couch and he wasn't there. I dropped to my knees and let the tears come. This was so much harder than I ever imagined. It hurt so much. I was trying to be positive, trying to stay focused on that he is here, but my mind was tired of fighting the negative thoughts that kept popping in. No wonder people stayed in bed; no wonder people wanted to give up. I wanted to hug Frosty and cling to his physical body, but he wasn't physical anymore. I was. I was still looking for that body, something tangible to hold. How do you hug a spirit? At that moment I wasn't sure. I was feeling that it wouldn't be easy.

I sat there crying over the seat where Frosty's physical body had once been. I just let myself cry and in the crying came a familiar calm, like someone hugging me. I didn't want to be hugged by anyone but Frizz. I wanted to pull away, but the thought came to my head: *It's me. I'm still here. I am still here.* I stopped crying and looked up. I listened and knew what I was feeling and who it was. I dried my eyes, blew my nose, and hugged the space in front of me, knowing he was there. The knowing was definitely easier than the not knowing. I breathed in the relief and the calm of him being there. I pushed myself to get up, turn the van on, and push in the *How to Be Happy* CD. I sat for a minute thinking about how amazing life is and how God really does provide a way for us to deal with all things. I couldn't help but wonder why the words *I'm still here* seemed to be screaming so loudly in my ear.

I was getting tired, so decided I would head home. I was almost there when that little voice popped in again: go *to the cleaners first.* I didn't want to go there as the guy who worked there sometimes asked about Frosty. I intended to avoid talking about him with as many people as I could. The voice pushed harder: *to the cleaners first.* Damn. I got to the parking lot and grabbed my things and went inside. The guy was there and we chatted for a minute, just catching up, with me playing the game that everything was good. I was having a hard time listening to him and what he was saying. I thought it was because of my grief, but I realized it was because I kept hearing a dog barking. At first I thought, *Wow, now it's in my head and it's so loud. I can't hear anything else.* The guy kept talking. I couldn't stand it. I interrupted him, asking "Do you hear a dog barking?" He said yes, it was his sister's dog. I asked if the dog was normally at the cleaners. He said the dog was normally in the back and he didn't know why he was barking and so excited. A small grin started on my face. I asked, "Where is the dog?" He said, "On the other side of the counter." I was expecting to see a dog that looked like Frosty, but when I got around the counter, it was a small miniature version of him. He was the same color and face shape, but small. I laughed and said to the furry friend, "What's going on?" I really was not into being around other dogs at all, and in fact I hadn't wanted to look at any dogs. This one was really calling to me. I got closer and the dog started jumping up and down and barking more and twisting in circles and pulling on the leash that was keeping him attached to the chair. It made me laugh. The man from the cleaners said, "Gosh, he never acts like this. I could feel Frosty's spirit talking to me, and it was like he was right there in body. I kept hearing, "I found you, Mama, I found you. See, I'm still here."

What a gift to feel Frosty so strong and to hear him so clearly. I thanked God for reminding me to ask for signs; those signs kept me going. Feeling Frosty now, even stronger than earlier in the day, made me so grateful I'd listened to that little voice when it said *go to the cleaners*. It had all been worth it!

Now I'm not saying that any of this is easy, but I am saying that those moments of feeling Frosty, and any loved ones in spirit, make this grief process easier. The signs bring in the joy, and when you are grieving, well, can there ever be too much joy?

∾ CHAPTER 27 ∾

*T*he next day was Saturday. It had been a week. How could that be? Only a week? In some ways it seemed like a lifetime ago, and other ways it seemed like it hadn't happened at all. But it had. It really had happened. It was never supposed to happen; Frosty was always supposed to be here. I wanted to stay in bed. Funny how my emotions can be so up one minute and down the next. I just wanted him back. God was going to bring him back, right? Let me just go back God, just give him back to me in body, just one more year with him, or even a month. Give him back to me in perfect health so we can go do all the things we used to. How easy it was to go back to begging God, pleading really. I had tried the bargaining thing before, but, in the state I was slipping back into, giving it another try seemed like the only thing I could do at the moment.

I kept watching the clock, thinking about where I was last Saturday, feeling the panic, reliving the moment, wanting to go back, hoping for that miracle. It had all been a dream, a nightmare, and now it was over and I was going to go pick Frosty up and bring him home. Please, God, just make it be a dream. It was never supposed to happen like this. When Frosty's time came, it was supposed to be in good health, in his sleep. The tears were rolling again, leaving me wondering when this grief was going to stop.

One of the hard things with our loved ones who have been sick for awhile before their transition is that our memories are of them being sick. We see them like that, remembering them in their illness, which is painful to see. We remember their pain and their discomfort. We want to remember them in healthier, happier times, but those aren't the most recent memories. I could relate now to other people going through that and talking about seeing their loved one for so long as sick. That picture is the way they were when we last saw them. It was so painful to look at the recent pictures of Frosty, that had been taken just a few days before his transition. I wanted to look, yet I didn't want to look. I wanted to see him before he got sick. I wanted to see him healthy, happy, and pain free. Frosty had only been really, really sick for the last four weeks, but he had been sick for almost a year before his transition date. I have great admiration for those who take care of loved ones year after year in their illness. I know now how much courage it takes to see our loved ones like that.

I pulled out pictures of Frosty that I wanted to see—pictures that would help me visualize him in his spirit body now. His spirit body is healthy and strong and goes back to a time about six years ago when we were hiking, running, playing, and going to the beach a lot. He was strong and fast and we would race each other to see who could keep going the longest. Of course Frosty would always win and not because I let him. I forced myself to see him like that, to embrace that image of him and to carry it with me. It was a struggle. My grief kept jumping up to cover me from seeing his now happy spirit.

So it's been a week. What now? It seems like that question was coming up a lot these days. I wasn't sure if I could go through with the day. It was another fake-it-till-you-make-it day. The plan was for me to spend the day with a friend whose brother had recently transitioned. He understood so it made it easier for me because he knew his brother was still here. Saturday was harder for me than it had been the day before, or the day before that. I was wearing down. It was normal, I knew. I was at the it's-been-a-week mark. It was also the mark of me running out of patience for Frosty being gone. I was ready for him to come back.

We went to a metaphysical bookstore first to do what they call the light table. It's a table that helps to align the energy points throughout the body. My friend went first, as I had done it before and he was anxious to get started.

When it was my turn, the man running the light table walked back with me to set things up and make sure I understood everything. I could feel Frosty loafing along beside me. I was grateful to feel him so strong. The man was ahead of Frizz and me as we walked in. If the man could feel or see Frosty there, he didn't say anything. He showed me where I could put my coat and purse and suggested I take my shoes off. There was a low table along one wall that had bottles of aroma scents on it. He picked up one and sprayed it. The other he had me sniff. He said it helped to open the senses. He put the bottles back down on the table and crossed the room to set up the CD player.

As I sat down on the light table, one of the bottles fell over and rolled on the floor. I tried not to laugh, knowing it had been Frosty's tail, so to speak, or his spirit tail, knocking it over to let me know he was there. The man turned around and crossed the room to pick the bottle up and, as he did so, he said, "Weird." I didn't think so. I knew what had knocked it over. I tried to hide the now growing smile on my face, not wanting the man to think I was laughing at him. Even though I had known Frosty was there, the added validation of him knocking the bottles over was priceless to me. I know I've said it before, but we humans just love that physical validation. It's the human part of us that needs that. The spirit in us just knows and accepts. What a wonderful gift.

How amazing it was that he had been able to get my attention. I knew it was possible, but it's so different when it's happening to you. It's almost hard to believe, and I'm sure some of you are thinking, *No way*. But think about it. Really stop right here and think for a minute. When was the last time you were drawn to something that reminded you of your loved ones who have transitioned? Think about it. Maybe at the time it didn't make sense, but now, thinking about it, maybe it does. Well, that was them. It was them. It was one of your loved ones in spirit, trying to tell you, *I'm still here. I am with you right now.* Maybe you couldn't see them, but I'll bet you could feel them and your gut was saying it was them, but you didn't want to believe because it wasn't possible. Right? But it is and it happens all the time. They send us all kinds of things in tangible form to feed that human need we have for physical validation. Those signs come from anywhere, from anyone, at anytime. All you have to do is be open to them and believe and it opens the door to receive more signs. Our loved ones appreciate acknowledgment just as much as we do! I thanked Frosty for his hard work and made a mental note to keep asking.

The next day, Frosty sent me more signs, but this time they came through my friend Artemisa.

Artemisa came to the park on an occasion to hang out with me and Frizz. The times we had gone, she was amazed at how many bluebirds always showed up to hang out with us. She said bluebirds represent play, fun, and laughter, and that they now would remind of her Frizzy. It had been about a year since her last visit with us in the park, but I always remembered what she had said about the bluebirds. Amazing how things really do happen in divine order. It'd been eight days since Frosty's transition and she was calling to tell me that she had just come out of a building early that morning and, much to her surprise, were sitting two bluebirds. She immediately thought of Frosty and knew they were from him. She was very excited and said he was telling me that he was with you and he wanted you to play, play, play. I was once again laughing through my tears. I could feel his spirit so strong through her as I remembered that day when she was in the park with us. I remembered how fast Frosty ran and how much he loved the bluebirds. He would chase them just enough to make them fly, then step back and watch them soar!

Having Artemisa tell me about the bluebirds also reminded me of a time when Frosty was about five. We were in the back yard and I was on the phone and he was doing his usual rooting in the dirt. There were always birds in our backyard and that day was no exception. The birds never seemed to be afraid of Frosty. I never understood why until that day. A baby bird had been learning to fly, so it was for the moment on the ground. I turned around just in time to see Frizz pick it up in his mouth. It took me a minute before I could even open my mouth to say anything to him. I was so stunned. I said, "Frizz, no, drop it!" I was a little uptight because after all Frosty was a hunting dog. He looked at me in that calm, cool, collected way that he always did. I said, "Drop it." He looked at me like, *What are you getting so uptight about?* He lowered his head to the ground while keeping his eyes on me. When his chin reached the ground, he slowly opened his mouth and the baby bird came out chirping, completely unharmed and just as happy as if it had been in the mouth of its own mother. I laughed and pounced on Frizz, wrestling him to the ground. Our new friend flew away to join his brothers and sisters. The seagulls were another of his favorites, but more about that later.

∾ CHAPTER 28 ∾

*I*t was now Sunday, one week and a day, and still counting. Gosh, it seemed like it had been forever, yet other times it was like I was just waiting to pick him back up from the vet's office.

I was supposed to go to dinner today with a girlfriend. She knew Frosty had been sick, but that was all she knew. I was feeling a little overwhelmed with all these people babysitting me, grateful but overwhelmed. I knew that wasn't what they were doing, but at times it felt like that. The constant reminders of Frosty wanting me to go play helped, but I just couldn't help but feel sad.

I was feeling tired and shaky from the lack of food and sleep and all the crying, but receiving the bluebird message told me Frosty wanted me to go. I would go for him, because he wanted me to and because the play seemed to help keep me open to feeling him around me.

Tami (not her real name) is an animal person like me, so I felt more comfortable about meeting with her. The plan had been to have dinner and then shop for a few clothes, and then she was going back to work. She worked at one of the big department stores so she knew her way around, which made it easier to shop. She was another one of my friends bugging me to get some clothes. What's wrong with T-shirts, shorts, ponytail scrunches, and running shoes? Frosty always knew when I put on my shorts and running shoes that we were headed out for a run in the park. Tami and I grabbed a light dinner and then picked out some clothes and headed to the dressing room. Once in the dressing room, I started trying on clothes and she was talking to me about work. I had been doing fine, but something she said cracked open the façade I'd been putting on for myself and everyone else. I started to cry. She said, "What? What?" When I looked at her, she knew. I couldn't get the words out at first, but then I said it. We sat for a minute, neither of us saying anything. She put her hands to her face and said, "Oh no." Then she jumped up and hugged me. We said nothing after that. What was there to say? She had some idea of what I was feeling.

I was suddenly very tired. I sat there feeling like a limp noodle. I just wanted to go home. No, I wanted to be with Frizz. I wanted to put my arms around him and bury my face in his fur and pretend none of this had ever happened.

Tami, sensing a need to change things up, started hanging up clothes and straightening up the dressing room. She was making an attempt to bring me back up, but neither one of us wanted to admit that. She suggested we go look at some of the new makeup in all the purple colors that were in. I was thinking how is eye shadow going to help, but I was too tired to ask and I knew she was trying to help. Purple was a color that Frizz and I had in common. I looked at the purples, found one that seemed fine, and handed it to her so she could ring it up. I was standing there thinking about Frizz and what we would be doing if he were here in his human body. To fight off the sadness, I started asking for another sign from him to show me he was there with me. A snow globe that was on display caught my eye just as Tami was handing me the receipt for my purchase. She said, "Let's get you a bigger bag." I walked over to another counter with her, forgetting all about the snow globe. She handed me the bigger bag with my purchases in it. The bag was screaming at me! I lifted it up and looked at the outside of the bag and I started to laugh. The bag was a seasonal bag with bluebirds on it. I heard a very loud screaming in my head—"Hi, Mama!"

I gave Tami a hug and headed out to the van. I couldn't help but notice the sheepish grin on my girlfriend's face as I left. What did she know that I didn't? I walked toward the van, suddenly feeling alone again, like Frizzy was gone. I knew he wasn't, but it was funny how fast those feelings came on.

I got in the van, going to the back to sit down next to the couch. I willed myself to focus on him. Gosh, I was so tired. I never realized how tired grief can make you. The thought popped in my head to look in the bag. I didn't want to. I just wanted to focus on Frizz. I sat there wishing he would appear on the seat, so I could hug him. Again the thought came to look in the bag. Why should I look in the bag? I knew what I bought. I argued with myself, not realizing the thought was coming from someone else. After about five minutes I gave in and went through the things in the bag. There inside was the snow globe with a bluebird hanging from a perch right outside its little house. It was the same bluebird snow globe I'd been looking at inside the store. My girlfriend had never known about Frosty and the bluebirds. There was only one way she could have known.

The happy tears started to roll and I thanked Frizzy for his work in making it all happen. I called my girlfriend and thanked her. She said it was weird how the thought came on so strong and so fast. I told her about Frosty and the bluebirds and thanked her for listening to her intuition. What a great day and so awesome to have Frizz in the store shopping with me. I forced myself to hold on to this feeling for as long as I could; I knew it was only a matter of time before my grief surfaced again.

On the way home, I thought how well our loved ones know us. It had been Frosty and I'm sure other loved ones who had pushed me to go shopping. He knew where I would go to shop. He knew the store I would shop at had the theme of bluebirds for that Christmas season. I could see how hard it was to stay in that place of believing Frosty was with me. My ego, my human side wanted me to believe that he wasn't. Funny how our egos don't want us connecting with our loved ones in spirit and no wonder, our loved ones in spirit are living in the light. That's what in spirit means: light. My ego wanted me to believe Frosty was gone. It didn't want me connecting with him, which meant I would be pulled into the light. That fearful human part of me would be left alone and abandoned, which wasn't true. Frosty was working hard to tell me and show me that he was with me, that he was right there. He was even coming into the department store with me. He knew I would go there. Like the song says, "Nobody knows me better!"

The sun had come out in my heart again, only this time, for the moment, I wasn't going to fight it. I realized I had been fighting against the signs that he was trying to give me. Gifts from Frosty, and I was rejecting them. I had been putting a lot of energy into wallowing in it and feeling sorry for myself.

I understand everyone goes through this and I wasn't putting any guilt on myself this time but just realizing how it could be different, how we can all make it different for ourselves. I'm not saying that we shouldn't cry or mourn the change that has come about. I'm saying that if we could look at it as a change, not a loss, and if we could open up to the idea that our loved ones are still there with us, just in a different way, we could experience some of the joy they are feeling at their transition. We would be more able to feel what they are feeling. How many times when our loved ones are here in human form do we disregard the efforts they are making to say, "I'm here and I love you"? We all do it; we're human.

Through our loved ones' transition, we have another chance to see them and their love for us. Some of them have to work really hard to get us to slow down and notice and I had been no exception. I worked as a psychic and I was missing or blocking out the signs. Frizz was working overtime with me and through my friends to give me bluebirds. I bet he wanted to knock me upside the head! Well, we've all been there and done that. The bright side is that we can open to the signs now. We can believe in what we know in our hearts to be true, *now*. Our loved ones are with us. We can feel it, and we can feel them. Don't let anyone tell you differently.

I wanted the signs and I believed in them, so I decided from that point on I would cry when I needed to cry and the rest of the time I would look for the joy and the light that Frosty was working so hard to send me. That was easier said than done, but it was a start, a willingness to at least be open to the joy and the light when it came my way. I wanted to be open because it was coming from my sweet precious Frizzy.

∾ CHAPTER 29 ∾

*T*he days kept passing as they do and so the nine-day mark came—yes, I was still counting. I wanted to pull the covers over my head and just hide. I knew Frizzy was here. I could feel him, but I still wanted to go numb. Funny how we make part of our human experience, an experience of shutting down. I love Frizz and having him in spirit, going now wherever I go, is a gift, a miracle, yet I was still shutting myself off from him. Why was I doing this to myself and to him? Why would I want to wallow in my grief? Why couldn't I see the chance for celebration and joy? Why was I taking away from him by not celebrating with him? The only answer I have is that I am part human, part spirit. experience. The human part of me wanted to wallow.

I can see Frosty wants me to celebrate. He keeps sending me bluebirds and funny movies and laughter. Why was I going back to the grief? Why did I want to? Just yesterday I said I wasn't going to do this anymore. But here I was slipping into that black hole of depression again. It's the place where my mouth freezes up and my lips become sealed shut. The self-pity closes me off from feeling him and from seeing him. *God, why am I back here? What have I let go of today that I had yesterday? What is so different today? Today, right now, I'm alone.* At least that's what I'm telling myself. I give up. I want to go back to bed. I'm so tired. The grief is so exhausting. I had a right to go back to bed; one day wouldn't hurt. I was giving up. I was entitled after all, because everyone, including me, had expected to be carrying me off on a stretcher by now, well before now. Frosty and I had been inseparable for sixteen years; five minutes of self-pity wouldn't hurt anything, not that I hadn't spent more than five minutes feeling sorry for myself.

As I was falling asleep, thoughts of Frosty and me on the beach popped into my head. We loved the beach, the water, and the running. Frizz loved the seagulls. In the Oxnard area, furry friends were allowed on the beach as long as they were on a leash. It meant the person holding the leash had to be able to run like the wind or fly to keep up with him. He loved to run as fast as he could, and it always seemed like he was trying to work up enough speed to fly. He would work up speed and then push off like he was trying to soar, but he never got off the ground. Well, maybe a little. He would be pulling so hard on the leash that it was like your legs were going to buckle trying to keep up with him. He could do it for hours and never get tired. When he wasn't chasing them, he would bark to them and they would squawk back at him as if they were talking. I would say, "Frizzy, you can't communicate with the seagulls. You're a dog." He would look at me with that "I'm bored" look. Of course he was talking to them!

The local beaches became a Saturday hangout for us and at least once a month we would go to Oxnard; later it became San Diego. We loved the beach and we always came back feeling very connected to the universe and our loved ones in spirit. If you're missing a loved one and have a desire to connect with him or her, go to the beach. It will open you right up and reconnect you with the all the ones you love.

Falling asleep thinking about the beach helped me a lot. It brought me some healing and I felt more joy when I woke up. I'd been feeling so alone when I went to sleep, convinced that I was alone, but I knew I was anything but alone. Why did I keep telling myself that? It wasn't helping anything.

My girlfriend texted me that I should go see *Tangled*. She didn't know I'd already seen it. I texted her back saying I saw it. She said, "Go see it again." How funny, but before I could shut down on the idea, the thought came that maybe there was a reason. I still wasn't back to work, so other than me wanting to mope there was no reason I couldn't go. So I put on my fake-it-till-I-make-it face and got up to get dressed. I headed for the closet to grab some clothes and out of the corner of my eye I saw a golden flash with a stuffed toy hanging from his mouth. My sweet Frizz had shown himself to me again. I had been open enough to see the flash of him, and he had pulled back the clouds and poured in rays of light and once again I felt Frosty's love. Gosh, was I grateful. God has poured the gift of intuition into all of us so we can communicate with our loved ones in spirit.

I'm not saying all this is easy or that it happens as fast as it sounds here. I have the same support system as everyone else, but working as a psychic has opened my eyes to believing that our loved ones are here with us and that they are trying in lots of ways to get our attention. They do tell us things and give us guidance. We don't hear, because we don't get quiet enough to hear them. Let's face it: we humans are not the quietest group of species. We are constantly in motion. We are fast paced, loud, and the more of it, the better. We go to psychics because they are quiet. We pay them to listen to our loved ones, desperately shifting from one psychic to another till finally we hear the message our busy minds have been screaming at us. We hear it because in going to all those psychics, we too have to be quiet to sit in the session. We've gotten quiet enough to hear what our busy minds by now are screaming at us. We are now quiet enough to hear our loved ones and the message they bring to us. Are we afraid to connect? Is that why we turn up the volume, or are we just afraid of love?

It's been almost two weeks. I still can't open my journal, touch it, or even look at it. Doing that brings on so much pain. The idea of writing anything down is more than I can bear, but writing is something I've always done. I don't remember when I started getting thoughts of writing all this stuff down. I filed it in the back of my mind, but it keeps coming closer. I kept asking myself how could I write any of this down? Maybe I could write a little and beat around the bush with it. I'll think about it.

I haven't answered e-mails or been online in weeks and I'm not looking forward to it, but it's something I can do without having to talk. One of the e-mails is about a workshop that involves psychic work and one I had heard about a few months back. I stopped going to workshops because I wanted to spend my time with Frizzy.

This workshop called to me a little, but I just wasn't ready. I deleted the e-mail and figured if it was meant to be then it would pop back up again, and it did only an hour after I deleted the first one. My first thought was, *Man I am being pushed hard.* What was wrong with me just sitting in my room for the rest of my life? I didn't want to go. I wanted to spend some time with Frizz. I wanted him back in body.

I knew I was supposed to go, but I didn't want to. I started looking for excuses to show the universe I had tried, but it just wouldn't work. I said, "Okay, I'll go, but only if I can take the van." No way was I renting a car. The van sometimes was an issue for parking because of the height. I called the person in charge of the location and said, "The parking is covered and has a height clearance, doesn't it?" The woman on the other end of the phone hesitated and said, "No, it's open parking." I said, "You mean it's not in a structure?" She replied, "No." I racked my brain to think of another reason to back out. I asked, "Well, how many spots are there that are not underground?" She said, "Three hundred parking places are open with no height clearance." Oh good, that would be my way out: not enough parking outside. I asked, "How many are registered for this event?" She said, "Three hundred." Yahoo! I tried, but there wouldn't be enough parking. Now I can't go for sure. A little voice said, "Not everyone will be driving there. People will come two and three to a car." She said, "Do you want to register now?" I said "No," and hung up.

The event was only two days away. There would be plenty of parking. I didn't want to go. I wanted to stay home. I wanted to be with Frizz. There had to be another excuse I could use to get out of going. Why was it so important anyway that I go to this one? Why was it feeling like the push for me to go was coming from Frosty himself? What other reason could I give to the universe to get out of going? Oh, yes, too short of notice for any of my friends. They would already have plans and I wasn't up to going on my own. Two names popped in my head. One worked as a hairdresser; workshop was on Saturday. Bummer. That took her out and let me off the hook. Another friend's name popped in my head: no worries, he never answered his phone. But I figured I would call just to save face with the universe—you know, show that I really tried. Hooray! I could stay home. I dialed my friend's number to show good faith, relieved that I wouldn't have to go. Oh my gosh! He answered on the second ring with an over-the-top cheery hello. Damn it. I told him about the workshop, throwing in that I knew he couldn't go but I just thought I would mention it. He said, "Oh, no, actually I am available and it sounds wonderful!" Great, not only was he available, but he was excited about going. I could almost hear Frosty laughing.

Fine, I said in my head. I gave up and called the workshop coordinator back to reserve our spots.

∽ CHAPTER 30 ∾

The park had been on my mind a lot lately. I missed being there, but I missed being there with Frizz. The idea of going without him hurt, but the idea of never going hurt, too. I knew never going again was not an option. Frosty would not want that. In fact he would love to go with me now, I was sure. His spirit would really soar at the park and mine would too. Was I ready for the pain that I was telling myself I was going to feel, or could I make myself open my heart to the joy that was there for me? The park was always a place that could do all of that for me and Frizz. I decided the longer I put it off, the harder it would become and I might not ever go back. That would hurt Frosty and it would hurt me.

Pulling in through the gate, I wanted to leave. This had been a bad idea. I just wasn't ready yet. What made me think I could do this now? It hadn't even been a month. I went to the area of the park that was always our favorite. It was where the grass would pool up with water when it rained and the seagulls would migrate there. I sat frozen, not wanting to get out of the van. It felt like a betrayal to Frosty by being here. I sat there thinking, realizing how wrong I was. He *was* here and probably barking at me to get out and go for a walk. I wasn't without him. This was surely where he would be. I pictured him standing outside the van with a toy in his mouth, telling me to quit moping and get out and run.

I forced myself to open the van door. Gosh, this was not easy. How did people get through stuff like this? I grabbed a couple of his toys and dragged myself out. I picked up his leash, which was always in the pocket of the door, and a bottle of water for him and the last stick he had chewed on that was still in the van. The tears began to come faster, blinding me from seeing what was in front of me. I stumbled slightly and I dropped one of Frosty's toys, which made me cry harder. I wanted to sit on the grass and cry my heart out, but I didn't want anyone to see me and I didn't want anyone to know how much this was hurting me. People saw Frosty as a dog; they didn't understand how hard this was for me.

I turned back to the van, putting all of Frosty's things back except his leash. I slammed the van door and told myself to stop thinking and just walk damn it, just walk. I took a few deep breaths and then started talking with Frosty as if he was right there with me. Sounds crazy, yeah, well, people could think I was crazy. Fortunately the park was pretty much empty, which is the way it usually was. I willed my mind to open to him and whatever else God wanted me to hear.

I passed one of the trees I always hugged for grounding and stopped to hug it then. Hugging a tree is very grounding and I knew I needed all the help I could get, besides it was one of the fun rituals Frosty and I always did in the park. I would hug the tree while Frosty started grabbing sticks from under the tree. When I was done, the stick wrestling would begin. I would start grabbing the sticks he had found and he would start barking for me to give them back. I would run with them and he would chase and lunge at me, biting at me. Once I did, Frosty would start the game of convincing me to let him take the stick or sticks home with him. He would head back toward the van carrying the chosen stick, prancing along with his head held high. Once in awhile I would let him, or pretend to let him, take the sticks, but then trade him for a treat once we got in the van. One day he found a stick so big he couldn't pick it up. He could barely drag it, but he was bound and determined to get it back to the van. The stick was actually a branch that had fallen off a tree in a recent storm, but Frosty was sure it was a stick and that he could carry it. I couldn't stand to say no, as he was so enthusiastic about carrying it, so I picked up one end with my hand and he had the other in his mouth. Together we carried the big stick. When we got to the van, he barked with excitement, telling me we'd done it!

As it turned out, the *stick* was way too big to put in the van and too thick for me to break a piece off, but Frosty was so proud of himself so we just hooped, hollered, and hugged anyway, and of course Frosty always loved that!

Going back to the park for the first time with Frosty in spirit was not quite the hooping, hollering experience it had been in the past with him in body, but it did help. Heading back to the van, I felt him with me and being in the park helped some of my grief to heal.

Leaving the park, to meet a friend at Knott's Berry Farm for dinner, it felt as though something in me had shifted. I felt more peace and more calm. I was beginning to believe that I might be able to do this and be okay. Once again, I was hopeful. As I was pulling out of the park, I said out loud, "With you and God helping me, Frizzy, I can do this."

I pulled into the parking lot to Knott's Berry Farm and my girlfriend who I was meeting for dinner called. She was running really late and would be there in about forty minutes. It was just as well because I wasn't hungry or in the mood to eat. So I said, "Let's just reschedule." I was feeling really good just being solo with Frizz and I wanted more time where I didn't have to talk with anyone. I was enjoying the peace that had come over me. I decided it might be nice to get out and walk a little. The night air felt good and helped raise my spirits even more. I was actually feeling happy, something I didn't think was possible, especially not this soon.

The first shop I walked into was decorated for Christmas. Oh God, how was that possible? I hadn't even thought of that. Nope, nope, I wasn't going to think about that. This year there would be no Christmas. I made it through Thanksgiving and now here was Christmas. I would just tell my family I wasn't doing it this year. It was just too hard. I'd been feeling so good before I walked into the store, but now I was fighting to hold on to that feeling. Christmas was just one more thing I would have to muddle through without Frosty there in physical form. I took a once-around the store, deciding to leave. I just wanted to get out of there and get back to the feeling I had when I walked in.

At the back of the store, in the corner, was a little place that had a few seats for people who were trying on shoes. I was suddenly feeling so weak and tired that I needed to sit down. I sat looking at the shoes and boots, thinking about

Frizz, and a pair of moccasin boots caught my eye. One of the sales girls came just as I saw them and said, "Can I help you?" I hadn't really intended to go into the store to shop, but the boots were screaming at me. I gave the girl my size and she went back to get them. I wondered why the boots were even screaming at me because I had nothing to wear with them. The girl came out, saying she had one pair left and it was my size. I thought, *How funny is that?* I slipped the boots on and they fit perfectly. I walked toward the center of the store as the corner where the shoes were seemed dark. I wanted to see what color they really were. I got into the light and realized that the moccasins were the same color as Frizz! They were another sign from Frizz that he was with me. Frosty was working so hard to help me get through this and show me he was here. I wanted to give back, do something for him. I didn't know what, but there had to be something. I knew being happy was what he liked, but in my human mind I wanted to give more. I just didn't know what.

❧ CHAPTER 31 ❧

*E*very day I made sure to ask for signs that Frosty was with me and every day the signs came, signs to make sure I was paying attention and kept paying attention. Some days it was harder to see them, especially the days that I was more focused on grief and shutting myself down against the joy of knowing he was with me. Some days I felt angry, so angry, and I wanted to hate the world, the vet, God, and especially myself. I knew it was really me I was mad at most, but projecting it onto others made surviving it all easier in that moment. On those days, I didn't feel Frosty as much and it was harder to see the signs he sent or I missed them altogether. It would scare me and I would force myself to practice gratitude for him and the things we shared and the gift of knowing he was there.

It was a couple of days before the two-week mark when in the mail I received another hello from my sweet Frosty. One of the Hallmark ornaments for 2010 was a bluebird. One of my girlfriends had gone into Hallmark and there it was, along with one of the Willow Tree ornaments: The Angel of Friendship ornament. If you haven't seen it, it's an angel holding a golden retriever puppy. Of course I cried and it hurt a long with the joy that came with it. The next day another girlfriend brought to me pictures of Frosty and me that she had taken just a few days before his transition. It was painful to look at the pictures, but it was hard not to look at them.

I took all those things as reminders that he was still with me, that our love was binding, and for his sake I continued to fake it till I made it.

The day before the workshop, I decided I just couldn't go, that I wasn't ready for an all-day class in a room full of people. My girlfriend Melissa made it her job to convince me otherwise. She came and took me for a pedicure and said many times throughout the day that Frosty wanted me to go, that it was all in divine order, and there was a reason I was going. I traveled between guilt, grief, anger, and back to guilt again. Gosh, that guilt is a killer. Melissa pointed out that I wouldn't want Frosty to sit home and mope. Actually I would, but that was my humanity talking. In the end, she convinced me to go, another fake-it-till-you-make-it experience, but my ego kept saying, *How can you be off playing when its only been two weeks?*

The morning came to go and the convincing I had received the day before had died in my sleep. This had not been a good idea. I was tired already and I kept thinking about the crowded room of people and my need to cry when I needed to cry. My friend showed up happy and ready to go. We climbed into the van and I pushed in the *How to Be Happy* CD and pretended I was happy and Frosty was sitting in the back of the van, going with us. It took awhile, but I started feeling better and looking for positives in the day. It was a workshop that involved psychic work. The people there would believe as I did, that Frosty was still there. The person I was going with had always been Frosty's favorite chef, so I wouldn't have to spend my day hiding my feelings.

The workshop featured James Van Praagh and Debbie Ford and a surprise visit from Cheryl Richardson. James and Debbie together was bound to be filled with laughter, fun, and personal growth. I found myself swinging back and forth between being okay with being there and reprimanding myself for not being home mourning and grieving. I was sure Frosty was thinking, *How dare she be off going to something like this? I bet she's glad I'm gone.* That hurt worse and I forced myself to believe that he wanted me there, that the workshop was going to bring us closer. It was hard to trust myself. After all, I had not known to be there when Frosty transitioned.

The workshop got underway with me swinging back and forth between fear and love. The meditations helped me make the shift; the writing assignments I avoided. I still hadn't done any writing. As the morning got underway, I began to feel calmer and more centered. The continual sobs that had been screaming in my brain for the last two weeks quieted down just a bit. I caught little glimpses of Frosty lying in the aisle next to me a few times and I was comforted by that. He had a way of keeping me grounded that always made me feel like I was home.

When it was James's turn to teach us, he started off saying that everyone would take something different home from the workshop. I don't remember all that he said because I zoned in on one thing that screamed at me. He said, "Some of you have started a book and will be inspired to finish it. Others will start a new book." Wow, I had been getting the push to write Frosty's book and I had dabbled in thoughts of writing it. I smiled to myself. Why would Frosty want me to write a book about him? What was it he wanted the world to know? I hadn't told anyone what I was thinking of doing. It was a very private thing and I wanted to keep my ego out of it as much as I could. I was afraid if I talked about it with people that they would try to talk me out of it and the idea was too fresh in my mind. I'd been sitting on it waiting for validation that I should do it—I guess I had just gotten that.

At the lunch break, my friend and I decided to use our time to go for a walk. We both liked the outdoors and neither one of us was into having lunch so off we went. As we walked, I couldn't help but notice that there was plenty of grass for walking Frizz and we even passed a park. I started thinking that I could have done this workshop easily with Frosty. The parking was close to the building, with plenty of breaks to check on him. There were places to let him out and time to do it in. Why hadn't God allowed him to stay longer? Why had he taken him when he did? What difference would two weeks have made? I could have gone to this workshop and had him with me. I stopped going to workshops because of the time I was giving up but also because it had gotten harder with Frizz slowing down. I didn't mind. There would always be other workshops, but this one I could have done with him. I was feeling the anger coming up again. What was God thinking anyway? Did he want me to be angry and mad? Why couldn't Frosty have stayed around until after the holidays? God must know how painful it was going through the holidays like this, much less any other time of year. I wanted to scream and yell and beat on something. What had God been thinking and what was the plan? Funny how the anger would come up out of nowhere so quickly. I wanted to go home. I didn't want to be here walking around houses decorated for Christmas, pretending that I was doing fine. The walking did help to let off steam and distract me from my anger, but those questions I knew would linger long after the walk was over.

We headed back to the church where the workshop was being held, when I saw a house with big red poinsettias planted throughout the yard. I was drawn to it so I turned toward it. I don't know what made me say it, but I did, "That yard needs a dog." We walked up to the big gate surrounding the yard, and down the steps came bounding a black lab that looked to be about a year old. My friend, being a furry soul lover as much as I, reached through and started petting him.

I stood frozen, not wanting to touch him, which was very unusual for me, but I just wasn't ready. The dog kept turning back to me, furiously wagging its tail. Finally, not wanting to disappoint the soul in the furry body, I reached through and let him lick my hand, just once. That was all I could do. My heart was breaking and I stepped back. I walked on ahead with the tears streaming. *I miss you Frizz. I miss you being in your body. I know you're here and it probably is you trying to tell me hello, but I just can't stay here. I don't want to pet another dog, not now, maybe not ever.*

Back in the workshop, we were led through some meditations and personal growth work. The day ended with a phrase that I'd already gained a belief in prior to this workshop but it was validating to hear it again. We were told that we are all spirit. We are all spirits here on earth having a human experience, and since we are all spirit that means that we could talk to other spirits, those in body and those with no body. As a child, I learned it's written in the Bible that Jesus appeared to people after his passing. Yes, I know that was Jesus, however in the Old Testament it's written that Samuel appeared to a woman who summoned him after his passing. Is the Bible telling us that living people talked to people who were dead?

The workshop was serving me in the form of validation for a lot of things. Ever since I can remember, talking to people who were in spirit was a normal thing to do; they were the same to me as people who had a body, and I always talked to them in the same way. I figured everyone talked to everyone, including souls in furry bodies, so why had I been doubting that Frosty was with me?

The workshop spurred me on to start writing, not in my journal but to write this book. My desire was to do it for Frizz because I felt like he wanted me to. I was guessing that he, like me had a desire to share with people that their loved ones are still with them, that we can talk to them the same as when they are with us in body. Opening up to the possibility that our loved ones are with us relieves us of the overwhelming feelings of loss that we go through when people release their body and move into traveling in spirit.

❧ CHAPTER 32 ❧

*I*t's been fifteen days. I can't stop crying; I'm not sure I want to. It hurts so much and I want to go back. *Please, God, just let me go back. I said I can't do this. I miss him too much. I know he's here with me. I can feel him next to me, I can smell his fur, but the human part of me won't let me go to that higher place. The grief is overwhelming. I've been trying to ride it out, but it's been a long day and once again I am left wondering if there is a God and how could he even consider having me do something I said I couldn't do.* I told God I couldn't do this. My sobs get worse and begin to overwhelm me. Why can't he still be here with me in body the way it was, just through the holidays, just for another couple of months? Why was it so important that he had to go now?

My heart feels like it's cracking down the middle. I wonder if people can actually get to the point of crying themselves out, to where they can't cry anymore. I thought yesterday's workshop was going to take all this pain away, but it seems to have brought up more grief. My family and

BETHANY-ELIZABETH FAYE HANSEN

friends think I'm okay, but I'm getting tired of pretending and now I'm worn out. The mental focus it takes to get through this is exhausting. I've been crying for two hours. I'm thinking a pill of some kind might be a good idea about now. How do people do this?

Some of my friends think I should be done grieving because it was a dog. Sixteen years is a long time to be spending twenty-four hours a day with anyone; there is attachment and there is love. I slide to the floor grabbing the Kleenex box and notice a small pile of dog hair on the carpet. I am so grateful for those little mounds of dog hair. My sobs slow down and I take a breath. That old comforting feeling moves over me and settles in my heart. I am grateful for the ability I have to feel him so close. I remind myself that when I don't feel him it's because I have stepped away or closed myself off. I remind myself that our loved ones in spirit are all about joy, happiness, and love. I feel so much better knowing he is there. I climb into bed with the smell of his fur, and I realize that it's going to be another night of sleeping on the edge of the bed. And I am just fine with that.

All this sounds so easy here on paper, but is it and does it happen quite that fast? No, but I'm sure if you have a loved one who you wish were still with you in earthly form, you know the grief. Whatever type of body they were in you know it's not an easy journey. We all know about the crying, the heartbreak, the dark lonely sleepless nights, stomachaches, anger, grief, and guilt. We've all been there. We're all very familiar with that part of our loss.

It's the joyful parts that we struggle to connect with that are the hardest to let in. It's the parts that we tend to push away. It's the joy in our loved one's presence, that angelic love that he or she is trying to share with us that is the part for us to focus on and put more energy into. It takes work and it isn't easy, but it can be done. We can choose some joy to go along with our grief. We can choose some love to go along with our fear, and with those choices the signs and messages from our loved ones will keep coming to comfort us. The more open we are, the more signs we are able to see. I've seen some of these signs throughout my life, so most of them don't shock me, but I'm always amazed at what lengths our loved ones will go to, to get our attention, to tell us they love us and that they're still here.

Asking for signs could be the easy part if any of this is easy, so I asked every day, well, every minute. Loved ones have been known to do all sorts of things to get a message to us. Frosty was no exception. Many times a day something would appear and I love sharing those stories because they brought me joy and his message of *I'm still here*. Any and every contact we get from our family and friends in spirit is a miracle of love. It's a miracle that they can send them and that we can receive them. There have been many signs from Frosty and they all mean the world to me, but there are a few that were over-the-top, out-of-this-world amazing! It really shows what our loved ones in spirit will do and can do to show love.

It had been a little over two weeks when I was feeling that push to go to the park again. Normally I would have resisted but this time I gave in and just went without putting up a fight. I was not looking forward to the pain I expected to feel, but I knew I would feel better after I went. I kept telling myself I didn't have to expect pain. I could expect joy.

When I got to the park, I spent some time walking, some time crying, and some time just being quiet, but mostly I focused on being open to Frosty and feeling him with me. By the time I left the park, I was feeling some much needed peace and I was glad I went.

Once home, I still had the normal unloading of the van to do. I was still taking Frosty's things with me, plus mine, so I usually made two or three trips back and forth and this time was no exception. I was on the second or third trip with my arms full, ready to step out of the van, when I heard it. I stopped and waited. I didn't hear it again, but I was sure of what I had heard. It was a bark, just one, but I knew it was Frosty. I stood there for a minute, then my doubt took over and I told myself it was a ball of his with the recording on it of him barking. I dropped everything and searched the van for the ball. I knew it wasn't in there, but my humanity was trying to talk me out of what I had heard, pushing me for a logical explanation, which was funny coming from me.

To me it would be logical that anyone could hear their loved ones, so why not me, and why not now? I always had before. I sat down in the van taking in a big breath and pulling in what had just happened. When I exhaled, it hit me. I cheered and yelled, "Yahoo!" to Frizz for his efforts and to let him know I had heard him. I had heard him and

I was going to accept it. I felt joyous and happy. My mind kept saying *Yeah, right,* but the divine in me knew what I had heard.

It got me thinking, about how many times have we thought we felt, heard, or saw one of our loved ones in spirit. It happens all the time, so why do we doubt it? For many years I was afraid to admit the things I had seen. What are we afraid of?

Another far-out sign from Frosty was the sudden appearance of a necklace. I woke up one morning and there it was. I felt some fear when I first saw it. I had never seen it before, but curiosity got the best of me and I got up and walked over to where it was hanging. It was a necklace like you would get if you won the Olympics. It was on a bright blue strap, the same shade of blue that had been popping up for a while now. I picked it up and turned it over to see if there was something engraved on the back and there was. I stared at it, as the tears of joy started to fall. Printed on the back were the words "Miracle Worker." For months I'd been praying for Frosty to be restored to perfect health. My friends said my prayers had been answered and, well, yes, they had been. Frosty was now in perfect health. I hugged the necklace to me, praying a thank-you. I put the necklace back where I had found it and left it there. It helps to remind me that miracles do happen when we believe.

∾ CHAPTER 33 ∾

*T*he signs were getting more convincing. I found that asking and believing in the signs that came made a big difference. The more I believed, the clearer the message.

Resistance played a big part in how easily I got the message and sometimes, even though I wanted the signs, I was still resistant to the information that came with them. The message that Frosty was still with me and still acting as my spirit guide, only now in spirit, had to do with a picture that I'd been carrying around. It was a close-up of Frosty in the park licking his chops after scarfing down a McDonald's ice-cream cone. It was one of the few in-hand pictures I had at that time. I kept it in the folder with the pen and pad I was using to write each night.

It was late one night and I got out the folder, the pen, and the pad to do some writing, but the picture wasn't there. I started panicking. I knew it had to be there somewhere, as I had been using it just that morning. I started going through the room, then out to the van and back to the room. By the time I got through, both were a mess and it was well after midnight. I could no longer think straight. I was exhausted from all the frustration, the crying, and the searching. I figured looking for it in the morning would be better, and surely then I would find it.

I fell into bed, still sobbing. Frosty was gone and so was the one good picture I had of him. The others were on my phone or in a camcorder. How could God do this? Yes, I was so angry. I wanted to blame someone and God was a good choice. I didn't realize how much anger I still had. It all came pouring out and it didn't matter anymore what I said because he had already taken Frosty. So I looked at it as if I had nothing more to lose. Yes, I had definitely hit my limit. I was beside myself with grief. I finished my prayer of anger now feeling a little calmer, and as I was falling asleep, the thought came to me to put on my grief CD. Funny, my daughter-in-law had said the same thing earlier in the day. I didn't want to. I was still mad. I would do it tomorrow. For years I had listened to motivational CDs and they always helped. They were one of my survival tools, but that night I just let myself hit rock bottom. I was too exhausted to care.

The next morning I got up early, hell bent on finding my picture, and I was sure I would. God knew I couldn't take anymore. I tore the room apart again and then started on the van. I went through the house and even the trashcans thinking maybe I'd thrown it out with some papers. Hours later, and lots more tears, still no picture. I spent the day going back and forth between crying and being angry. I kept thinking, *Why would God allow that picture to disappear?* I was getting so angry and worked up that the grief would roll over me, overwhelming me. In my moments of being slightly rational, I understood that it was just a picture and that I still had Frosty with me. But I had already lost so much. I knew I was thinking irrationally, but in that moment I couldn't help it. I was just too worn down.

I called a couple of my friends asking if any thoughts came to them as to where the picture might be. A couple of them said take a break and it would show up. My daughter-in-law again said to put on the grief CD. Melissa, my girlfriend who'd been working on her psychic skills, said it was between a cardboard-like flap in my room. By the time I got home that night, I was so frustrated. I knew looking for it would probably not result in me finding it. I was too tired. I fell into bed another night crying my heart out. As I was falling asleep, the thought again came: put on the grief CD. Again I told myself I would put it on tomorrow.

It was now Friday, the third day since the picture had disappeared. I had a couple of appointments that I couldn't cancel, so I did my best to let go of my now growing obsession to find the picture and get on with the day.

When it was time to leave, I started my ritual of loading up the van. I opened the front door and there was a package on the doorstep. I was still too upset about the picture and since I wasn't expecting anything I left it there as I was going back and forth. I intended to leave it there and let someone else pick it up. On my last time out to the van, I thought I better put it inside. Leaning down to pick it up, the package felt soft. I knew my family in Utah had ordered a blanket with Frosty's picture on it but it couldn't be the blanket. We were told it would be six to eight weeks before delivery and it had only been two. We were hoping it would be here in time for Christmas, but with everyone shipping presents we thought it unlikely. Deciding it couldn't be the blanket, I took the package with me, putting it on the back couch in the van. I would open it later.

When I finished my first appointment, I climbed in the van and went to the back. I remembered the package and sat down to open it. It was one of those do-you-laugh-or-cry moments. It was the blanket from my kids in Utah and it was a picture of Frosty sitting right where I was on the couch in the van. The picture of him was larger than life, and I mean big! I knew it was Brandon, who I lovingly refer to as my adopted son, who had done the actual ordering. Everything he does is done with pounds of enthusiasm. It's one of his gifts. I laughed through my tears, picking up the phone to call to say thank you.

Brandon answered on the first ring. I told him the blanket was here. We've always teased each other, so at first he thought I was kidding. But knowing that lately I had not been in the mood for games, he hesitated before saying anything. I said, "Really, the blanket is here." He was stunned. I described the blanket to him, so he knew I was serious. He was as excited and as happy as I was. He kept saying, "I can't believe you got it already!" I said, "The picture of him is the same size as Frosty. How did you get it so big?"

He laughed. "I told him I put it in the back of the van on the couch where Frosty always lay." Looking in the rear-view mirror, I could see the blanket just like I could see Frosty when he was back there. Brandon laughed again and said, "See, it's like he never left." Hearing that was music to my ears!

What a miracle the blanket had arrived so fast. It was just shy of two weeks since it had been ordered. How could it have gotten to me already? God and Frizz had sent me another gift, so I guess I had to stop being mad about the other picture of Frosty in the park, just finishing the ice-cream cone. I felt a lot better, but honestly I still wanted the missing picture back. Getting the blanket helped to shift me into gratitude and calm me down. When I went to bed that night, I grabbed the cardboard case that my grief CD was in and laid it next to me so I could use it for my meditation in the morning. I swallowed down some Nyquil, yes, Nyquil. I wasn't a drinker, but I was so tired yet couldn't sleep. The Nyquil would make me go to sleep.

In the morning, I felt better. I had actually slept. No wonder people drink when they go through the grief process. I remembered the grief CD and leaned over to put it on. I flipped open the case and there inside was the picture of Frosty in the park, the one I had been looking for. How could that be? At first I was confused and then I started to laugh.

The message had been coming to listen to the grief CD. It came to me at night when I was going to bed. My daughter had suggested it to me three or four times. My girlfriend Artemisa had said for me to keep acknowledging the grief. If only I had followed the guidance … If only.

My girlfriend had been right. She told me it was in my room in between a cardboard-like flap. The whole thing was just another reminder for me to get quiet and listen. I could see that the grief had taken over again. I know everyone has grief. Grief is a normal process, but I was fighting it. Recently I heard a great saying from an angelic lady who facilitates a grief support group. She said, "Grief expressed is grief diminished." The way I was processing or not processing the grief was creating a barrier in me, so I needed to express it, and as soon as I did I felt better, more open. Releasing and expressing grief allows for an opening into joy, so, if you are feeling grief, have a good cry and then open to joy and you will feel your loved one around you. They never leave. It is we in our grief who shut down and turn away.

My girlfriend, her two kids and I went to the park to celebrate her birthday. Before I left the house that morning, I asked Frosty to show me how he flies. I asked him to be close to me and give me lots of signs, as I was meeting them in the park where Frizz and I always went. I was concerned about how I would feel and be. We took the kids on the swings and the climbing bars, and then we decided to take them for a walk. In the past, when I was there with Frizz, there were always butterflies and bluebirds around us, so at first when a butterfly showed up I didn't think too much of it. We took our walk and the butterfly stayed close and went with us. That was getting a little eye raising because we walked for forty-five minutes.

When we got back to the car, we sat on the back tailgate drinking water and giving the kids something to eat. The butterfly was still there, so I walked over to it and said, kind of jokingly, "Come on, Frizz, show me your stuff." My girlfriend is a firm believer that our loved ones are with us, so she was going right along with it. I lifted my hand so the butterfly could land on me. It was only a minute before it came. As it sat there, I was filled with amazement. I could feel angels surround me and my heart opening. Frosty was showing me once again, *I'm still here.*

The butterfly was miraculous in itself, especially since this picture was taken the second time the butterfly came back to talk with me. However, if you look hard enough, in the background you will see a lady walking a white dog! How amazing our loved ones are.

~ CHAPTER 34 ~

I ask myself, *Why do I keep writing all this down? Why don't I just start journaling again? What is the difference?* I realize there are reasons I'm writing it all out. It's in the writing that I am realizing that looking at death, and seeing death from a different perspective, can and has helped me get through a time that could have been oh-so-much-harder. It could have been a time that was joyless, but the truth is there have been many moments of joy. I wouldn't have been as open to them if I wasn't faced with the words on these pages every day. I always had the perspective that our loved ones are still here. I've seen it firsthand, but when it hit in my own backyard, so to speak, it was very different. I was seeing it and feeling it through my own eyes. Is this the first time in my life I've had to go through this? No, in fact some loved ones in my life who have transitioned could have been, should have been much harder.

I can't tell you why Frosty's transition has hit me harder than the others, but it did. What I can tell you is that having those moments of joy helped to heal me and see the benefit in what I had been telling myself about death. Hanging onto grief was easier, more familiar to me then letting it out. Crying was not my thing, but then singing praises of joy really hadn't been either. I found that it's the joy and the love that connect us and it's the joy and the love that heal us, and that is what our loved ones are trying to tell us.

It's a back-and-forth thing, but choosing to allow some joy in gives the option of going back and forth instead of staying in the grief and maybe getting stuck there for a long time. It wasn't easy, but I saw how holding onto the grief and not releasing it blocked the signs of things going on around me, before and after Frosty transitioned. I missed what was happening because I was focused on the grief of losing Frosty, of having him die. I held onto the grief so hard it turned into fear. Fear showed me one thing: love would have brought me another.

Realizing I chose fear over love, I used that to pile on guilt, beating myself up for what I had not seen. The guilt blocked signs too. *Well, now that I've opened the door to guilt, I might as well swing it wide open. Do I know guilt? Yes, I know guilt. I've had lots of it, a lifetime of it.* I found the guilt was a bigger blocker to connecting with Frosty and my other loved ones than the grief was. Guilt called for punishment and that meant shutting myself off from those I loved, those in spirit and those in body. At times I jumped into it with full force, withholding from myself and or beating myself up. Other times I found myself in the middle of it, only stopping when

I realized I had shut myself off from feeling Frosty. I would remind myself of what my teachers taught me, which is that guilt is about awareness and learning, not about beating yourself up.

Knowing guilt, you'd think I would know guilt and be done with punishing myself after the first time, but it doesn't go away. It comes back. That human side of us brings it back over and over again. I was aware of those guilt feelings and still there were times when it came back to jump me in the dark. I would begin running again, turning on the TV, eating, shopping, unaware that my guilt was back running the show. It would be two or three days of missing Frizz so much that I would finally give in to forgiving myself. With guilt I had to forgive, forgive, and then forgive some more. While kicking myself and holding onto guilt, I closed myself off from seeing the signs or even thinking to ask for them, but it didn't mean the signs didn't keep coming, because they did.

A few years ago, I used to keep Frosty's yellow ball in the van. It was a ball with a recording of Frosty, my oldest son, and me playing. There was a period that the ball would roll forward constantly, right up to my feet so I couldn't push the gas pedal. The thought kept coming to slow down, but I wasn't convinced so I took the ball out of the van. A clear sign to slow down.

One of my girlfriends called me about a dream she had about Frosty dying. When I heard the word *dying*, I told her that was something I wouldn't talk about. Six months before

Frosty transitioned, birds, mostly doves, kept showing up on my porch, in my yard, and one even in the house. They all transitioned into spirit shortly after they showed up, or had already transitioned when I found them. In one of the animal books it says call on the dove when someone you love has transitioned, because the dove can help you to connect with your loved one.

Another sign came just five or six days before Frosty's transition. He stopped wanting what I ate. That was a sure sign, especially for someone who was in a doggie body. I blocked it, ignored it, or tried to. My gut was screaming, but I was not going there. Frosty was going to live forever and that day was never going to come.

My fear continued to override the signs. When Frosty was born, I noticed a blonde angelic lady with the energy of an angel. She was in spirit. I assumed at the time of his birth that the lady was his guardian angel, but when she showed up again, just a couple of weeks before his transition, I forced myself to deny who she was and why she was there. I wanted her to be there for someone else or for something else.

One of the more obvious signs was my monthly calendar. I always used a daily agenda book, along with a monthly calendar. Both calendars stopped on the day Frosty transitioned. It looked as if life stopped after that day. I usually filled things out four to six weeks in advance, but there was nothing on either calendar after that date.

It would be so wonderful if I was over and done with guilting myself, but I can assure you that's not the case. I still allow the humanity in me to punish and withhold, but now I know it's up to me to be ready when the signs come. If I focus on me and continually go within, I am more ready to see those events in my life through eyes of love. I then have the ability to change how they happen. I can make them happen with guilt or with love. I can perceive my loved one's transition as a time of grief and guilt or I can receive some moments of joy and love, for they have evolved. In their evolvement, I can evolve too. I realize that I am here to learn lots of lessons and all those lessons go back to learning about love. I had to learn love. That's what Frosty tried to teach me and has now succeeded in teaching me.

It's love that breaks down all barriers to everything and everyone. It's not time but love that heals all wounds

It's been a little under three months. It's been a confusing time. I feel like I've been on a teeter-totter. I don't know what I want. It's like coming when you're going and going when you're coming. It's like walking on hot coals. It's hard to look at his pictures; it's hard not to look. It's hard to be in the van and it's hard not to be in the van. The bedroom is painful and yet comforting. Sometimes I'm laughing and sometimes I'm crying. At times I can't stand being alone and I feel desperate to be with people. Other times, being around anyone is just too painful and it brings on more pain. The hot coals get hotter and harder to walk on. Sometimes it hurts so much, but I know I have to keep going, even when I don't want to.

I do feel and see him here and he continues to let me know he's here, but the human side of me still wants him the way he was. I look at his pictures and it kicks me in the heart that I haven't seen him in so very long. I'm not used to that. I was with him every day, every minute. He went where I went. I want him back the way he was so I can hug him again, tell him I'm sorry, and go back and do it over again. But above all else, I know he's still here.

I feel him, but it's different and I'm not good at different, even if it is for the better. I guess resisting is part of the lesson and clearly I am clawing my eyes still a lot of the time. I knew there was a better way, but I put up such resistance. Debbie Ford says, "What you resist persists," and damn is she right.

I wanted to go to the park, but it hurt when I did and it hurt when I didn't. In the end, I knew the hurt would transform itself into love if I went, so I did and I came away feeling joy. It's talking yourself past that hurt that is the hardest, but, once you do, look out because love *will* shine through.

It'd been raining so much, which was unusual. Parts of the park were closed off to cars so I had to park and walk around to the part that Frosty and I loved best. It was the part where the shade trees, the water, and the bluebirds all came together. It was also the part of the park that flooded the most when it rained and right now it looked like a shallow lake, so much so that there were lots of seagulls standing on the edge of it. The seagulls reminded me of all the times Frosty and

I spent at the beach, chasing seagulls. The sadness welled up in me again and then the thought came to ask Frizz to show me that he was there with me, still chasing seagulls. Voicing it out loud, instead of in my head as I sometimes did, I asked him to show me that he was here.

I passed the first lake, willing myself to stay open and praying the seagulls would take flight. Standing at the first lake, nothing happened. The first bunch of seagulls just sat there in their little lake, not even looking at me. My thoughts started the back and forth thing in my head again. I wanted to cry, give up, and go home. I thought of what I had learned about planting seeds. The flowers don't always come up exactly when I want them too. I took a breath and moved on to the second lake. There were even more seagulls in that one. I started willing in my mind for Frizzy to show me something, anything, so I would know he was there. Funny, because as usual I could feel him, but I wanted more. My heart started to pound and, as it did, well, you can imagine what happened next.

There was a big whoosh and all the seagulls took off, becoming air bound making a big circle over my head and then coming back again. It was a big in-your-heart experience and I could almost hear Frosty laughing at the joy of it. I thanked Frizz for his efforts and his love, picked up the biggest stick I could find, and headed back to the van.

Yes, my heart still hurt, but there was good mixed in with it, along with the realization that heaven is right here. I didn't have to look up or reach for the stars high above my head. I simply had to just go within. What a great day and how lucky I was that at last the joy was catching up to the pain!

Another week went by and now it's been a month. How could it be a month? It couldn't be. I don't want it to be. I don't want to write anymore. It seems like a waste to be doing this. I want to run from my feelings and this writing is making me face them. It's too painful. Whose idea was it anyway to write this stuff down, and why am I doing it? I don't want to feel anymore and writing makes me feel.

It still always shocks me how fast this grief comes on and overtakes me. One minute I'm fine, sometimes even good, and the next I feel like a dump truck has driven over me and the grief and the tears come on full force. It's like being on a teeter-totter that won't stop going up and down.

No wonder my doctor offered me medication. Months ago, food would have been my drug of choice, but now it's too hard to eat. I can't eat, and if I could I would be afraid of using the food to block feeling or seeing Frizz.

I've heard people say you forget, that it gets better with time. Forget? Forget what? Forget him? Forget my other loved ones? I don't want to forget; I want to remember. I intend to remember. I want to connect, but it hurts. I'm afraid of the pain. I'm afraid of hurting so much. Up, down, up, down. Some of my friends have left, distanced themselves. They don't want to be reminded of their own pain. They don't want to see in me what they feel in themselves. I understand. I've done that too.

Christmas is almost here. More pain. I plan to ignore it. I don't want any part of it. I hear myself say to others, "Fake it till you make it." I hear myself say, *I don't want to.* I now see myself in them. I know I would be more connected to Frosty if I did fake it till I make it, but my grief has a hold of me now in a big way and I'm giving in to it. Sometimes I can fake it and I feel good. Those are the times when I know my heart is open to receive what Frosty is trying to give me. For now, my grief is overwhelming and it's going to take some time on my knees and the courage to cry. Why? Why does there have to be grief and why does it have to hurt so much?

CHAPTER 35

I worked for the first time last night. It's been one day short of a month. I hadn't planned on working, but another person who works as a psychic called two nights ago asking if I would. She had been hired to work a Christmas party for a local chamber of commerce and there were supposed to be two of them. The person scheduled to work with her had the flu, so now she was trying to find someone to fill in.

The party was in one of the beach cities that Frosty and I always hung out in. When she called, there was less than twenty-four hours for me to get something to wear, create a table setup, and prepare myself to do readings for two to three hours. I wasn't sure mentally I could do one reading, much less for a couple of hours. I told her I'd call her back in an hour. I had to think about it.

As soon as I hung up the phone, those fun little signs that you get when your divine support team wants you to do something started showing up. I got multiple signs from

Frosty to go. I headed to the mall to see if I could find something to wear, in the seventy minutes left before the mall closed. The sales girl seemed extra nice, going back and forth to help me in the small amount of time we had. Normally shopping for clothes is not my favorite thing. This seemed so meant to be: it was quick and easy, and I even found something in purple, which is my favorite color. I called the other psychic back, saying I would be there to work the following night. I ran around the next day getting the table set up, meditating in between stops, and trying to prepare myself for the evening to come.

The evening went really well and seemed fun for everyone. I was glad I'd done it. Yes, I had a little cry, okay, a big cry, at the end of the evening when I went to our place on the beach where Frizz and I always hung out. Standing there on the beach, I did feel sad, but along with my tears was also the part of me that knew I wasn't alone. I understood how much Frosty and others had done to get me to go through with that evening, to show me that I could go back to doing what I loved, when I was ready. The sadness I was feeling came along with feelings of peace and love, and for that I was very grateful.

∽ CHAPTER 36 ∾

*I*t seems like many people transition at Christmas time. Why is that? I've heard it asked many times before and now I'm asking myself that same question. I wondered about that before I went to bed at night. A piece of me wanted no part of the upcoming answer, that way I could shift back into my angry place and be mad at God and never feel this hurt again. I could just close my heart for good.

Thinking that through, there were a couple of problems with that. The first was I probably wouldn't feel Frosty as easily, because he is love, and only love and always will be. Closing my heart meant never feeling love at all ever. Maybe that wasn't a good idea. I still wanted to hold on to some anger. After all, God had taken Frizz right before the holidays. What kind of God would do that?

I woke up early a few days before Christmas with the answer clearly in my head. Christmas is a time, more than any other throughout the year, when the world is surrounded in divine love and support. It's like a blanket of snow covering everyone and everything with Christ's love. No matter where we live or who we are, the spirit of Christmas seeps into our hearts and turns us into love. At Christmastime we are considerate and caring. We go the extra mile to spread Christ's love and to support the ones we love. Love is what heals, so when I think about it, having someone transition at Christmas time is a gift for everyone involved. The love supports them in healing.

Wow. Okay, maybe God wasn't as cruel and unthinking as I was trying to make him out to be. I still wanted to be mad, to keep myself safe, but, now with this new awareness, I realized I wasn't keeping myself safe at all. I was hurting myself, Frizz, and everyone else I loved. I was now coming from a different place and that place involved love. Maybe God loved me more than I thought he did. That awareness alone changed my perception, helping to create a shift in me. Love seeped in whether I wanted it to or not. Did it turn out to be the best Christmas ever because of my new awareness? Well, I wouldn't go so far as to say that, my new perception did help me through it.

New Year's Day, brought with it the six-week mark. What was this New Year going to bring? I didn't know and I was pretty sure I wasn't ready for it. I was in transition just as much as Frosty was and just as much as everyone else who's gone through this kind of a change. I knew I was going to have to keep pushing or it would be so easy to just give up. I had fought going through Christmas and yet the signs just kept coming and I always felt better, but I still fought moving forward. With it being the New Year, I thought about my transition day and how long did I have in this body. I'd never been afraid of that before and I wasn't now either, but it was something I thought about.

My thinking was telling me to get dressed, get out of the house, and call a friend. Frosty wouldn't want me sitting here, thinking about my transition date, and neither would anyone else. I was better off thinking about what I was going to do for the rest of my life. Maybe I should think about what I was going to do for the day.

My brother came into town for the New Year, but I put off setting up a time to meet with him, I wasn't ready to tell him or anyone else about Frosty. I wanted to see him and I knew I could do the fake-it-till-you-make-it because I always enjoyed myself when we spent time together. My brother is also a doggie person and always looked forward to hanging with Frizz, but if we met in a restaurant, I could come late and leave early. There wouldn't be a chance for him to see Frosty. My girlfriend said just tell him. I said I couldn't. Talking about it still brought me to my knees and for the most part, only the people that saw Frosty daily knew about him.

I was still avoiding anyone and everyone that might ask. I realize not telling people could be a form of denial, and it probably was, but for the most part for me, it was such a private thing that talking about it was more than I could do. I knew at some point people would start asking, but for now it was between me, Frizz, and God.

The visit with my brother was wonderful and helped pull me out of my slump. He's a communicator with a sense of humor, so it helped to shift me into a fun place. God helped protect me from having to talk about Frizz, so when I left early I felt better for meeting him.

I was headed home when one of my sons called, hitting me up to go bowling. Bowling? Nothing against bowling, but I hadn't been in years. I thought, *What the heck.* Divine order, so I went with the flow. For those of you who haven't been bowling in awhile, the lights are now much brighter, the music is a lot louder, and the scores are much lower. Good thing we were there to have fun and not to win!

After that I was ready to head home. It had been a good day, but I was tired. Driving home I thought about how the people in our lives support us and don't even know that they are doing it. God really does send people to support us when we need it most.

One of my friends called just as I was pulling in the driveway. "Hey let's hit the movies, are you up for it?" I was ready to go home, I just wanted to be with Frizz—for a minute there I'd forgotten. My friend pushed, hitting me with the *Frosty can come too* phrase. She was right. Now he could. I was used to having him wait in the van, so there would be places I didn't go because my desire was to be with him. Now he could go everywhere, all the time! It took some getting used to, looking for him in places that he previously couldn't go, but it was true I was feeling him everywhere I went. I would forget and suddenly I would feel or see him and I would remember. A picture of a golden retriever would appear and I would stop to look at it with the feeling of someone being next to me or behind me.

I'm sure you've all had that happen where you feel like someone is there, you turn, and there's no one there—at least you think there's no one there. When it happened, the thought would come to me that Frosty was trying to tell me he was there.

I was so used to leaving him in the van with his toys, water, and windows open, and a big hug on the way out, but now he was right here with me. I just had to ask and pay attention to the signs. He was there when I needed him, showing up when I called on him. It had always been like that with my other loved ones in spirit. Times when I needed words of wisdom, my grandfather would come to me with his cigar lit. I would smell it before I saw him. He was always the same, standing there like he had all day, with that twinkle in his eye and a smile that was ready to laugh at any moment. All this with Frizz was the same. It was just closer to home for me than it had ever been before. I was struggling with more grief and surely more guilt.

The week after New Year's hit hard. The holidays had truly ended and I was left to figure out now what to do with my life. Friends and family were now back to work full force. More and more of my support had to come from me, which is the way it's meant to be because ultimately our grief is our own. On my own I found myself pulling up the guilt card more and more. During that time I still saw signs, but there were fewer of them because I'd turned away and closed off my heart again. I laughed less and I played less and, yes, I'd been to this place before. Anyone who's been through a loved one's transition knows about the back and forth. I felt so guilty, I hadn't been there for him, I let him transition alone in a cage. Why? Why hadn't I been there?

There'd been so many signs that life as we knew it was about to change. Why hadn't I looked harder, dug deeper to ask what the end result was going to be? I didn't want to see, the fear had been too great. I couldn't even begin to go to that place of seeing life without Frosty in his physical body. For life to be that way just couldn't exist for me. I wouldn't let it, even though I was familiar with what we call death. I had the validation, but I refused to go there in any way shape or form. I was so afraid of losing him, of him being gone, that I turned away from him. I had someone in my life that I refused to lose, to let go of. I didn't want to see. I chose fear over love, letting my fear shut me down, and close me off. I closed myself to love, and to life, because I was looking at it all through the eyes of pain. But it could have been different.

I could have made it different. I could have chosen differently for Frosty and for me. I'd never believed in death before, never supported the idea or the word death, but suddenly now with Frosty I was feeling what I had seen others feel. I now knew death, but it wasn't really a death, but I made it that way by clinging to my fear. I'd missed out on life because of the perception that I'd brought on myself and created in my own mind. My thinking had created my experience, and now I would have to redo my thinking and create something different for myself, and I had been working at doing that.

My mind wanted to overrule my heart at every turn. Now I had to make a choice and stick with it or stand to lose more of what I was saying I believed in and loved. I had to make a choice to be open to love and to look at things differently, hold on to what I had always believed in before, only now I was being pushed to stand in that belief. So what was my belief now that I was in this place? Well, it hadn't changed really, it'd just been my fear that had fought to get me to change.

I believe that everyone in our lives who we love comes to us from God. The people in our lives are gifts from God and God is love, so where there is love, there is God. Love holds everything and everyone together, so it would make sense that we would always be with the ones we love, whether they are in body or they are in spirit.

The thought came back reminding me again that we are their heaven. Peace and clarity were rolling upon me. I could see that true love means celebrating the advancement of our family and friends. It's a day meant to be celebrated. It's a day for transformation, not only for them but for us too.

In celebrating our loved one's transition, we have the opportunity to create a shift within ourselves, to choose love, and in so doing we let go of a lifetime of guilt, grief, fear, and all the what-ifs and the how-comes. With God's help we transform it all into love. We can open up to embrace love, with love, for those who we love.

Why was I so resistant to celebrating Frosty's transition, when in the past with other loved ones I hadn't been? Why was I putting myself through all that? Was I really perceiving this as a loss? I had never thought of it like that before, so why was I doing it now?

This wasn't the first person in my life to transition. Why was I filled with so much fear this time? Was the guilt causing me so much grief? But I had experienced guilt before. Was I afraid to go to that place of deeper love and connection? Clearly I was being asked to do that now. Was staying in the grief an easier thing to do, to punish myself with guilt than being in a place of love and joy? Is love that painful that I would want to reject it? Why wasn't I feeling more motivated to step up to a higher level of awareness? After all, it was connecting with Frizz that I was talking about.

Real love has the ability to celebrate the advancement of another. How willing was I to really love if I wasn't rejoicing in the advancement of those who I care about on their transition day? Moping around was easier in the moment, but over time it was pulling me from rejoicing in Frosty's ability to now be everywhere. Was the moping around and feeling sorry for myself so much more important than being able to have him still be with me?

Another week went by, bringing in comments from friends and family that it was time to get a puppy. That only brought me more pain. Some mentioned selling the van and moving on. That brought more pain. I knew they wanted to fix things for me. I understood their suggestions; I had done the same thing myself. Those who really understood said things like, "It's like a child or a partner transitioning. It will take time." And I knew they were right.

My girlfriend's mother transitioned just weeks after Frizz. It was a hard time for her too. We grieved together; there was no minimizing of my grief because Frosty was in a doggie body. It was easier to be around people who understood.

My spirit guide, my guardian angel, my protector, my partner, and my teacher were all rolled up into one. Frosty has always taken his job of teaching and guiding very seriously. His job was to teach me to trust my instincts and listen to my own inner voice the way he listens to his.

Sometimes I had no idea what I was supposed to be learning and I was sure only God knew what Frosty was trying to teach me. The one thing I was sure of early on is that Frosty *was* teaching me and that he was very committed to doing things the way God intended. I learned to follow Frosty following his heart, and I would always get the lesson. Through Frosty I learned love, which ultimately is God's love.

My life was filled with so much more and I became so much more because God chose the perfect teacher for me. Watching Frosty, I learned to go within, to get quiet, and through Frosty's transition I've learned the value in trusting God's plan. It will take time to adjust to this change, and it does for everyone no matter what kind of body the person you love was in.

I know more about grief than I used to. I now get that everyone deals with grief in their own way, with a common denominator of love. It helped to have Frosty's things around, to have the van with his toys in it. Those things helped to connect me to the joy and acted as reminders to ask for signs of him being with me. There were moments of pain when I looked at his pictures or held his things. The tears would come and go, but I always felt better afterward, with feelings of gratitude that I still had his things with me.

For me, that is what worked. Some days it was more damned if I do and damned if I don't. I just couldn't get away from the grief. Trying to get away from it made me hurt more. On any given day it was a minute-by-minute struggle to do what I had to do to get by. What I needed one day might be different than the day before. Everyone's needs, as well as mine, had a lot to do with how much time you spent with that person, how long they were in your life: did you talk with them every day, did you see them every day?

If there's guilt and unforgiveness, the loss seems deeper, more painful. Not being able to talk with them in the same way adds to our pain.

Learning the new language of spirit is a challenge, as is learning any new language. I was fortunate in that I was somewhat familiar communicating with people in spirit. I had learned it when I was young, so it felt normal to me, but I now had to practice it during the process of grief. It's all worth it though because at the end of our lives here in body it's the people, not our stuff, that we long for, live for, and love for.

It seemed as if everyone, no matter what their advice to me or what they had done in similar situations, seemed to have a natural knowledge that their loved ones were still around them. In the quiet conversations with friends trying to help, no matter their religion or upbringing, they all believed the same thing: it was only when they thought about what they had said that they would take it back. It's as if their natural God-given knowing would surface, but then their fear would rise up to meet them, making them rethink what they had said. It always seemed to me that the times when most people would look for the aid of a psychic would be after a loved one had transitioned into spirit. They knew instinctively they could connect, they just weren't sure how to begin nor did they realize that some of the things they noticed were signs from their loved ones.

I was grateful for the friends and family who stuck to their God-given instincts because it gave me the chance to talk about Frosty when I could talk about him, which wasn't often. When I did, it brought joy alive! One of my friends upon getting out of the van would continually yell out, "See you later, Frizz!" It made my heart rejoice every time she did it and it reminded me to keep asking for the signs of his presence. It was a gift of support that she gave me every time we were together. She showed me that where love goes, so do those that we love.

Now, I'm here in the park, thinking about Frosty's birthday that is coming up. I made it through Thanksgiving, my birthday, Christmas, New Year's, and now comes Frosty's birthday. I know even better now how it feels when someone talks about the first Christmas, or the first Thanksgiving or the first birthday, all holidays that are the first with their loved one no longer in body. It's a time of counting, counting, and more counting.

Frosty's birthday was something that was always a big deal, so now what? There was that question again. Sitting there looking at the lake, I knew Frosty would want to be near the water for his birthday. I smiled thinking about the first time he had made it into this very lake.

Years ago, a friend met Frosty and me at the park. My friend was excited about taking Frosty on the walk, so I let him hold the leash, forgetting to tell him about Frosty's love of chasing the ducks. He didn't know Frosty all that well, so it was truly a case of the dog being in charge. There were ducks all around and Frosty's excitement grew, pulling harder on the leash with each duck that showed up. I knew he would never hurt the ducks. For Frosty it was about making them fly, so the anticipation of seeing them soar was spurring him on and he began tugging harder at the leash.

I knew Frosty well enough—much better than my friend did—so I always knew when to pull back so neither Frosty nor I ever ended up in the lake, but by the way things were going, I was seeing that this could be a first. I was in the mood for some entertainment and as long as they were providing it and I stayed on the dry side of the bank, well then great! It didn't take long and Frosty was trotting closer to the water's edge and it was just about that time he caught sight of a big white duck—the white ones were his favorite.

The sudden motion of it coming down into the water made Frosty react without thinking. He lunged out at the duck, soaring above the water and landing in the lake. It caught him and my friend by surprise. The tug on the leash as Frosty lunged forward was unexpected and the automatic reaction to pull back left my friend teetering on the edge of the bank. Frosty in the meantime had never been fully submerged in water before, but it took only seconds for the retriever in him to begin dogpaddling to stay afloat. The look on both their faces was one I will always remember.

Frosty made it fine back to shore with my friend in a panic, thinking I was going to go off on him because my golden pup was now a brown wet mess. As he helped Frosty up the bank, I stepped forward and then realized more fun was on the way. Frosty always shook like crazy when he was wet. It was another humorous moment when his feet touched dry ground. He immediately shook, covering my friend in mud and water. He looked as though he had been in a rainstorm. We were all laughing by then and I said, "Guess Frizz is riding home in your car."

≈ CHAPTER 37 ≈

*C*elebrating Frosty's birthday wasn't going to be easy if I kept telling myself it was going to be hard. I asked often in prayer what I could do about it, how I could celebrate with him now being in spirit. I knew he would want to go to the beach. I wanted to acknowledge him and what he would want even if he were in spirit. Little articles started popping up in e-mails with the words "San Diego" in it. A friend from San Diego called. I couldn't go there, not without Frizz. Please, God, don't make me do that. It was too soon and too much pain.

I love Frosty and I know in that love he wants me to heal. I fought with myself for a week or so, going back and forth in my mind, arguing with myself. I finally stopped resisting and agreed I could try to go. I would at least get in the van and drive in that direction.

Once upon a time, I loved going to San Diego, but now I didn't know how I would feel and then there was the fear of running into someone who would say, "Where's Frosty?"

After deciding I would go for the day, I had to get some things out of the cupboard in my weight room. When I pulled the door open, out fell my suitcase. I knew right away what the message was.

My heart dropped. I couldn't spend the night down there, not without Frizz. We'd been going there for about five years. It was about three years ago that I met Dennis, the operation's manager. There'd been a problem with the room and he had helped me out. Ever since then he'd been putting Frosty and me in the same room every time we went. The room was set up in a way that made it easy for me to have Frosty there, having a bigger bed and double doors that led out to the park.

The last weekend back in September that Frosty and I were at the hotel was the last day Dennis was working there. Staying at the hotel would be hard enough, but being there and not being in our room seemed like an impossible feat for me to accomplish. I came to the conclusion that I would go, if I could stay in the same room that we'd always stayed in. If it was meant to be, then it would happen. I said, "Okay, Frizz, if that's how you want it for your birthday, make it happen."

I put a call in to the hotel manager who I had spoken with a few times before. It took a day or so before we were able to talk, but when we did it was clear that divine order, God, and Frizz were serious about making this happen. The hotel manager connected me to Chrissie, who finished up the reservation. Everything was set. Frosty was going to get his wish.

The usual back-and-forth within me started up. I felt excited about going and I felt pain about going. I knew we would be in our room—yes, it would be painful, but comforting at the same time. It became a reality for me the day before I was to leave. I started packing and the packing pushed me into a meltdown. I kept going to pack Frosty's food, his water bowl, and all the things that I always took for him. I was sure at that point I just couldn't go. I just couldn't do what was being asked of me. It was just too painful. When I went to bed that night, I listened to one my CDs, and prayed, hoping it would help me feel differently in the morning.

The next morning I woke up with a renewed sense of strength and knew I could do this, would do this for Frizz. It was that morning that I made a pact with myself to stop telling myself it was going to be painful. It wasn't helping nor was it making it any easier to go. I knew there had to be some joy in going and I intended to focus on that joy.

I was surprised the drive only took me an hour. Normally it was longer. I drove straight to Shelter Island to the hotel. It was too early to check in and I wasn't ready anyway, but I wanted to drive by to warm up to being there and going inside.

Driving past the hotel, I whispered softly, "We're here Frizz; we're home." I felt happy and sad at the same time. That was all I could muster up.

I headed over to Seaport Village, which is an outdoor shopping center in San Diego that's right on the beach. I'd only been there ten minutes when I ran into a friend. She'd never known Frizz so I was able to spend time with her without fear of her asking about him. We visited for about an hour and then I started feeling antsy to get to the hotel. It helped me to be out by the water, which cleared my head and helped to shift me into believing that I could do this. I headed back to the hotel, pushing in one of the motivational CDs. I kept looking in the rearview mirror, making sure Frosty's toys were all there.

The room was ready when I got there and had been for a while. I got the key and walked down the hallway with very mixed emotions. I wasn't sure how or what I was feeling, but I forced myself to keep moving. I could feel Frosty excitedly tromping down the hall next to me.

I opened the door to the room and stepped inside and just stood there. The room felt strange, like something was different. It took a minute to realize I actually was feeling okay. I headed out the other door to the room to go unload the van. I could still feel Frosty on my heels, which helped to bring a smile to my face. I started the unloading process and I'd made a couple of trips when I realized I was beginning to shut down, to feel numb. It was kind of like that feeling right before a storm hits.

It took me awhile to unload as I kept stopping and distracting myself. I knew I was putting off doing nothing. I knew what was coming and, when I finally got into the shower, the storm erupted and the grief of the past two months collapsed down on me. I finally hit the place of nowhere to go, no one to meet, and no way out of this. The tears fell for hours.

I tried to talk to Frizz to pull him in, but the grief was overwhelming and my mind was too exhausted to get to the place of even praying. I was surprised to find with all that grief how quickly the guilt came on too. It was happening all over again.

It was like the more things I thought of to feel guilty about, the more grief there was and the harder it became to cope or to hold onto my sanity. I was again asking, *How do people do this?* The strength that it takes to just put one foot in front of the other and keep going is a miracle in itself.

Happy birthday, my sweet, precious Frizzy! Once again, I'm fighting back the tears, but after sleeping for a few hours I do feel better. I thought about how different this would be if he was here in body. I dismiss that thought, trying to be happy for Frosty on his first birthday of being back in spirit. I know he wants me to be happy as do all our loved ones. He deserves to be celebrated. I pull out the waxed candle cupcake I got for him a few months ago, before all this started. I sit down on the bed next to all his things and I light it. The sobs come suddenly and I can barely breathe.

The day loomed ahead looking long and endless. Was it really only noon? How do people do this? How do they get through the grief? I got in the shower, washing the grief down the drain. I force myself to sit on the patio, knowing the sun will help me to feel better. I sat for about an hour, thinking I was feeling better but noticing I was avoiding

Frosty's things, which was not normal for me. I grabbed one of his toys and went back to the patio. I sat down and asked Frizz to show me something tangible. I knew he was there, I could feel him, but sometimes my humanity just pushed for that little extra piece of validation.

It was hard sitting there, just sitting there doing nothing. I was being confronted by my feelings. I kept looking for something to do to get away from it all, but there was nothing to do and nowhere to go, even my cell phone was strangely quiet.

This was the time God was giving me to feel my feelings with no distractions—well, almost no distractions. I remembered the vending machines in the hallway and knew there would be sugar there. I grabbed some change and headed out the door. I bought two candy bars, one to eat on the way back and one to eat when I got back to the room. It felt weird. I hadn't eaten any sugar in months. I finished the first one as I was getting back to the patio.

I was opening the second one when I saw him walking across the grass. I sat there looking at this golden retriever. Frosty was showing me he was with me. My heart pounded and I watched as if watching my lifeline. Maybe this sounds a little dramatic but seeing someone who looks like one of our loved ones in spirit always makes us stop.

Seeing that golden retriever reminded me that what I wanted most was to have Frosty there with me in body. The tears started up again. Gosh, was I having trouble creating a celebration for Frosty. I was now getting mad at myself.

I grabbed paper and pen and headed out to sit on the rocks by the water. The self-pity and the poor-me attitude were almost comical, considering all the gifts I was receiving today but unable to give any back.

I was in our hotel room. I was able to feel Frosty and he had already sent me many signs he was here, and I'd been given the opportunity to celebrate his birthday. And we were together. Yes, in a different way, but we were together. I couldn't help it, but I had to start because I was getting sick of the poor-me thinking that I kept pulling myself back to. Frosty had been working his butt off to help me and I was busy whining.

The rocks were overlooking the ocean of San Diego. I could see ocean for miles. I breathed in trying to relax my body and release some of the anger I was feeling toward myself. It's so beautiful here, how could I stay mad? I begin to surrender to what is and I felt a furry soul standing behind me. I turn to see if it looks like Frizz, but no one is there. I know it's him and, even though I can't actually see him this time, I can feel the look on his face saying, *Get over yourself.* He's not mad, just giving it too me in that wise way that he always does.

I'm beginning to feel calmer. I still miss seeing him in body, so again I ask for a yellow golden retriever to come to me. I, of course, expect one immediately, and when one doesn't come I ask for sea lions. Sea lions look to me like rubber dogs. They bark and they have ears that fold down. I wait a minute and no sea lion appears. This human stuff takes patience. I sit trying to meditate, while asking for the sea lions or the retriever to appear.

It's when I calm down and focus on my breathing that five sea lions swim in front of me. Isn't the world great! My heart is lifted and I do my best to acknowledge them, God, and Frizz. I make a mental note to look up sea lions for their meaning in my animal book.

It's almost dark, so I head back across the grass to my room. I get to the door and slide it open and something makes me stop and turn back. I turn around, and coming down the sidewalk toward me is a golden retriever. It looks amazingly like Frizz! I watch until the furry soul is out of sight, and then I step inside the door and the tears begin to slide. I wanted to let loose again and cry only happy tears, but the sad ones threaten to surface too. There's a song playing on the CD player that distracts me. Funny, I don't remember leaving it going or having that CD in. The player is belting out the voice of Julie Andrews singing, "Oh what's the matter with me?" The song stops me. She sings the line again and the light bulb in my head goes on.

What *is* the matter with me? I asked for sea lions and there they were, five of them. I asked for a furry friend that looks like Frizzy and two appear. I ask to be put in the same room that Frizz and I have always stayed in and here I am. I ask to feel him with me and here he is. I feel him. What is the matter with me? I should be rejoicing, I could be rejoicing. I could be expressing gratitude, because all this is a gift. I'm here in this place on his birthday and he's no longer in pain.

FROSTY MY SPIRIT GUIDE

All of this is reason to celebrate and now finally I am pushed into joy!

I light Frosty's birthday cupcake and this time I'm belting out the happy birthday song. Yes, I have tears rolling down my face, but these are tears of joy. I pull out the birthday present I got for him and I rejoice in the awareness that we are together with all our loved ones and that it's love that keeps it that way.

The next morning, while loading up the van, I ask myself the normal question, *Am I ready to go home or not?* I had done a lot of crying, but I'd also done a lot of releasing and healing. The quiet time had opened me up to a closeness with Frosty that I'd not had before this weekend. I realized I was feeling amazingly calm and happy. It was like his heart had grown inside mine and I couldn't help but think that this is the way God intends for it to be.

The van was loaded, but I wasn't quite ready to leave. It seemed natural to go for a walk as that is what Frosty and I always did before we headed home. It was almost noon, so there were a few people out walking and setting up blankets in the sun. It felt good to be out there walking and, true to recent form, I could feel Frosty walking next to me. I walked down the parkway on the grass instead of the sidewalk, knowing Frosty would prefer the grass. At the end of the parkway a mother was sitting on a blanket with her two little girls. One looked to be about four and the other one was younger, around the just-beginning-to-walk stage so I guessed her to be eleven to fourteen months. The younger one sat facing me; the older girl and her mother sat facing the beach. The little one was so cute and reminded me of my newest granddaughter. I was almost to the end of the grass, just passing them and the youngest one said, "Doggie, doggie, doggie, mommy doggie." She was pointing in my direction. I turned quickly to see what she was pointing at. There was no dog, except Frizz of course. The little girl's mother turned around and looked for the dog. She saw nothing and she said to her little daughter, "No, no, honey, no doggie." The little girl, being persistent in what she knew she was seeing, said a little louder this time, "Mommy doggie." She was still pointing in my direction. I grinned from ear to ear, saying to Frizzy, *She can see you!* I wanted to run over and hug the little girl and tell her she was right. That old saying *Out of the mouths of babes* popped into my head. How truly wonderful that God gives us so much through animals and children. Through them we learn to trust and believe.

After watching the little girl point out Frizz, I felt so exhilarated and joyful that I was practically running back to the van. I opened the door and hopped in, feeling that now familiar feeling of Frosty beside me in the passenger seat—no more sitting in the back of the van for him! A loud, *Roll down the window* screamed in my head and I laughed.

I drove off the island with a big smile on my face and my furry friend drooling out the window. Wasn't life grand?

Happy birthday, Frosty!

∾ CHAPTER 38 ∾

*S*omething in me had definitely changed over the weekend. I was feeling more joy and more happiness. Maybe this really is the way God wants it to be, wants us to be.

I felt and saw Frosty more, in a bigger way, like his presence had grown and become stronger. I thought maybe it was a combination of him honing in on his spirit skills and me communicating with him in this new way. But whatever it was, it made my heart sing and it made me want to share that feeling with everyone I knew who was grieving the transition of someone they loved. It was such a beautiful feeling.

It felt for me like heaven, which is what Frosty had been trying to share with me all along. This must be the feeling that our loved ones are trying to get us to open up to. What a picture-perfect plan God had created. It meant that we could actually create heaven on earth.

BETHANY-ELIZABETH FAYE HANSEN

It's now January 20. It's been two months. So much has changed. I'm no longer sure where some things end and some things begin. I've learned to surrender and to "Let go and let God." It feels as though I've been writing for so long, yet I still haven't opened my journal. It feels like I will stop writing soon, that all that I have written is close to a transition of sorts.

Transition is a word I've come to know and actually feel some love for, because of the different meaning it brings to replace some harsh words I was never comfortable with, before I started writing this. I was thinking the word *transition* and saying it, but now I feel it. I feel when our loved ones transition they are still living souls, and they are still here with us. Our loved ones release their bodies and gain the ability to be free, to move about, and to be everywhere, with everyone they love. Our loved ones are with us whenever we ask them to be.

I caught a radio show yesterday in which a woman was asking if the dog that is her companion and that she loves so much could be a substitute for a soul mate, the type of soul mate that you learn by and are guided by. The host of the radio show said, yes, and there's no *substitute* about it. He said some of our most valuable lessons in life come through our animals. I was surprised to hear him say that, as I thought I was the only one who felt that way. The show encompassed grief, and as I listened I realized how strongly I also felt about the presence of our loved ones being with us even after they transition and how important it suddenly was to me to have people know that they are still here. I realized I have a deep desire for people's pain to be eased and transformed into love, and the more I thought about it the more I wondered, *Is it my desire or is it the desire of all our loved ones who are trying to tell us that they're still her?* Frosty was going to great lengths to let me know he was around me.

I thought about connecting with Frosty and others I love who have transitioned and what it takes to talk with them. I had usually kept it to myself when I would smell my grandfather's pipe or my grandmother's cigarettes or the wave of peace and feeling of light that comes to me when Faye is near. Why was it so hard for me to admit the things I saw and to talk about them with anyone?

I'm pretty sure at one time or another everyone has smelled his or her loved one's perfume, grandma's cookies, or has seen a pair of shoes that reminds them of someone they loved. I know I'm not alone in suddenly feeling like there is someone with you. I was always hesitant to talk much about it. Frosty has changed all that for me, because now I see how much it really does happen. All I had to do was ask him to show me something, and he always did. I came to realize how easy it is when I practiced it daily. I can even look back now and see where with other loved ones I disregarded the signs they sent me. I didn't ask for the signs like I do now. One of the things I've said in the past, and of course I say it with Frizz now is how much I would love to have just one more hour with him. I realize now I don't need it because I have it.

At nine weeks, I'm back to not sleeping, and the anger is building again. I even get mad because I am tired of this up–and–down, back–and–forth crap! I wonder when it will end. Thank goodness the house is empty tonight. Everyone has gone out of town. It seems like there is more anger now than there ever was. How could I get so angry again? I'm tired of all of this. I want my Frizz back. How could God take him? Haven't I already been through this and done this too many times before? What will it take to be done with this grief? There has to be a magic pill or something to make it stop. I'm mad at God again. I scream at him and ask why he did this and why I had to go through this, like this. I don't want to scream at God, but I'm so mad and there isn't anyone else.

The lack of sleep, grief, and anger has pushed me into a place of being irrational. I throw things, wishing God would appear so I could yell right at him. I'm now mad at myself, because I'm acting so human. I don't want to cry anymore. I would rather be mad. It doesn't hurt as much. I scream some more and in my screams I ask if there really is a God and in my anger I forget about all the miracles that have come to me. I know there is a God, but right now I am so angry and hurt. The last few days have been good. Who flipped the switch? I want this grief to go away, I want no part of it, I hate it. I want to be done with it. I know that's crazy, but that's what I want. I liked feeling happy and watching for signs from Frizz, so why am I back here? It happens every few days. If there is a God, make it end and bring my Frizzy

FROSTY MY SPIRIT GUIDE

back. The anger builds, but it's funny how it builds against God and never against Frizz. I know some people get mad at their loved ones for leaving. I've done that with other loved ones, but Frosty has done so much for me in body and now in spirit that I never thought to get mad at him.

It's six o'clock in the morning and the whole night has passed. I'm too tired to be mad anymore and the grief is taking hold. The heavy sobs return like a storm that rolls in, hitting hard and then gently subsiding, seemingly on its own. This time feels a little different from the past. This time, the calm is there, but I feel the urge to get away from myself, to eat, drink, shop, or run. I feel a panic now and I hear my inner voice saying, *He's not coming back. Now what are you going to do?"* The truth is, I don't know what I'm going to do. It takes so much longer than usual to figure out what to do. I feel disconnected this time, but the solution does come: I'm going to talk to Frizz just like I always have, and he's going to talk to me.

It sounded easy and it always had been in the past, but this time turned out to be extremely difficult. It was like I couldn't reach him and he couldn't reach me. The anger was still there. I was still feeling it and holding onto it. The normal grief was there, but now there was grief about the anger and how I was feeling toward God. The guilt came up, creating a block. I felt guilty about feeling angry with God. It all just seemed way too much and I couldn't get a handle on it. I thought I was reaching out to Frizz, but I wasn't. I was doing it with anger instead of the way I had done it in the past. I turned the TV back on. I reached for the junk food and the sugar and stopped listening to my inner voice. I'd chosen the anger above all else. I had lost my connection, given it up so I could stay mad. I turned away from the pain and my connection to the divine. The more disconnected I felt, the louder I turned up the TV. My human voice didn't want me to reconnect, so it spoke louder than my spirit and louder than Frizz. The louder it got, the more pain I was in, and the more pain I was in, the more guilt I heaped on myself, and the more overwhelming the grief became. It was a vicious cycle I could see with my heart. It wasn't working for me, but my head had a hold of me and was convincing to say the least.

I was in agony. It was like losing Frosty all over again and myself at the same time. I knew he was still around me and I knew it was me who had shut myself off from him. He was still there with me waiting patiently for me to come to my senses. My biggest fear had become my reality. I had given up my connection with spirit. I was tired and grief stricken and almost hitting the place of no longer caring. My focus became the fear I was feeling. I suddenly lacked love and I could see the dark places I could go without love. My motivation to stay in spirit was to be and stay connected to Frosty and my other loved ones, which as it turned out I really did want more than I wanted to give up.

In the end, I turned off the TV and put down the food and stopped running from my grief. Yes, it was painful, but I had made it more painful by shutting myself off from

God and Frizz. I saw how easy it was to slip to that place of no connection and it really woke me up. How had I gotten so far down, so fast, and without me realizing what was happening? I wanted to know so I could be more aware. It was a few days I didn't want to repeat.

As I went to bed that night, I prayed for an answer as to how my anger got so out of control, so fast. In the morning my answer was there. My anger toward God had started it all. I hadn't resolved it and hung onto it staying mad. My anger made it easy to start putting other things before prayer, before meditation, before Frosty. I shifted back to doing meditations, slowing down and listening to my inner wisdom, and most of all worked harder on forgiving myself. I forced myself to focus on love, knowing that love was what gave me the ability to communicate with God, Frizzy, and my other loved ones in spirit, as well as my loved ones in body.

I'm sitting in the back of the van on Frosty's couch, thinking about the last few days and how much better things have been now that I'm seeing more clearly. I was alone with my thoughts when a face appeared in the back window. People did that from time to time when their curiosity got the best of them about the van. The window in the back is tinted so they would peek in trying to get a look, not realizing Frizz and I were sitting in there. This time it was a man peering in. I sat still watching him, wanting to laugh, finally I could hold it no longer and I burst out laughing.

The man was licking on what used to be an ice-cream cone from McDonald's—you know the low-fat kind that you could eat ten of and never put on a pound. Well, that was true in Frosty's case. Did you know it really is okay for souls in furry bodies to eat ice cream? Well, according to Frosty it's okay. He was about seven the first time one of my friend's came by the house with a McDonald's ice-cream cone. There is a McDonald's close to our house, so he would stop and get one and then swing by the house to say hi while still eating the cone. In the beginning Frosty would just stare, mesmerized by the eating of the ice cream, but, as time went on, Frosty decided, he was going to have some. So one day he put all his efforts into begging for a lick and finally he got one. I was against it because dairy really isn't good for souls in doggie bodies, but I was outvoted and, besides, as Frosty would say, ice cream does have protein and calcium in it.

Once Frosty got a taste, a pattern began to form. He started connecting this friend with the ice-cream cone and not just any ice-cream cone, but the one from McDonald's.

The bedroom faced the front, so Frosty could always see who was coming and going. When this friend came by, Frosty could see and hear him. He could be sound asleep, resting his head on the windowsill, and he would just know the ice-cream friend was there. One eye would flip open, then the other, and then he would spring into action. He would stand up and immediately start barking. Sometimes it seemed as if he was barking before he was fully awake. He was very verbal, so he would talk to both of us at once, telling the friend to hurry and telling me to open the front door. He was very loud and there was no doubt to anyone what he was saying.

Once I got the door open, Frosty would fly across the front porch, sliding by the time he got to the end because he was going so fast. It looked like he was on roller skates. It always took my breath away, but Frosty was in total control. Somehow he would time it perfectly by ending his slide right in the spot where the ice-cream cone would be standing. In the beginning he was allowed a big chunk off the top of the ice cream. It would smear all over his lips and face. He would lap it off quickly, looking for more, always wondering why the friend was now licking off the rest of *his* cone.

It was a game that kept us all laughing, especially when the cone was gone and Frosty would go back to say thank-you with his usual kisses and paw touches. The paw touches were his way of hugging you. Watching him go back and say thank you always reminded me to say thank-you. He was teaching gratitude.

The ice-cream treat turned into an even bigger game the first time Frosty was in the car to actually go through the drive-through when the cone was ordered. He was beside himself with excitement. We pulled up to the window to order and as soon as he heard the words *ice cream,* he stood up in his seat with that look on his face that said, *I'm about to communicate something to you.* He was loud so he would sometimes give you a warning, if he wasn't too excited.

We got to the pick-up window and the lady was already there holding the cone and waiting for the money. The car window was down, so Frosty could talk to her directly. He started talking furiously to the lady holding the cone. His tail was wagging, so she wasn't afraid. She was laughing. She was amazed at how excited he was, so she handed over the cone to him. He lobbed off most of the ice cream off the top. There was a second or two of brain freeze from the cold, and then the cone was gone. Poor Frizz, he was going to be sick, I thought, but no, it never happened. Frosty was fine. It almost seemed like it was his way of saying, *See, souls in furry bodies can eat ice cream.*

It didn't matter whether it was on a cone or in a cup—he always went for it. That same day, Frosty almost had his first shake. I left my shake in the cup holder of the car. The door that we were going into was locked, so we had to turn and go back past the car to get to the other door. It was a gift that the door was locked because, as we turned back, there was Frosty in the car window with my shake cup in his mouth. He had gotten the lid off and it looked as if he was drinking from the cup the way a human would.

We ran to the car and got there just before the shake was to pour out onto the seat. Fortunately for me and Frosty's stomach, not only did he have that enduring way of saying thank you before he ate anything, but he always asked before he ate whatever he had. He would pace back and forth carrying the object in his mouth as if he was asking, *Can I have this?* He hadn't received permission yet, so he actually hadn't swallowed too much of the shake. Lucky for me, Frosty was so polite all the time—well, most of the time.

∾ CHAPTER 39 ∾

The days have turned into weeks, and the weeks have become a few months. It's hard to believe and also scary. What if I forget? What if I wake up one day and I can't remember?

I could never before go to a place of thinking about Frosty's transition, and yet many times during the last year I prepared for it. Looking back now at some of the things I did do to prepare made me think of the divine order of things that helped to prepare me and all of us for the tough things in life. All the signs before and after were divinely driven with divine timing. I believe God and all my other Heavenly helpers were trying to help me and Frosty, and are still trying to help me. I can see that Frosty's true heart's desire is to stay connected, just as it's the heart's desire of all our loved ones. Sometimes it's more difficult than other times to see the connection and to keep it. The times when I found it hardest, Frosty would reach out through my friends, knowing they would pass things on to me. There were the bluebirds that two of my friends kept seeing and would call and tell me about. At Christmastime a friend brought a stocking with the caption that read "Thoughts of Home," which was part of a phrase I used in one of the games Frosty and I always played. The stocking had on it the imprint of a dog wagging its tail. The stocking came with a card with a picture of a girl dressed up in boots and carrying lots of colored bags. Frosty was telling me again, *Go play, have fun. Live!* Frosty was visiting my friends in spirit form, whispering in their ear to pass me messages.

I received a birthday card, just days after Frosty's transition, from a friend who I hadn't had contact with in years. The card was addressed to Frosty and me both, which was normal for people to do with us. It said, "Hope you two had a great day!" These people were unknowingly working through divine guidance not even knowing Frosty had transitioned into spirit.

Our loved ones work through others all the time, whether they are in body or whether they are in spirit. It doesn't matter what kind of body they were in, they all work for the same thing. They work to send us love and guidance. They are letting us know that they're here with us, right next to us. Yes, they are at a higher level of freedom and awareness, but they are here with us. We are their heaven. They want to be with us, just as we want to be with them. Their desire is to show us that it's about connecting in a new way, a way filled with more love, more forgiveness, and more joy. It is a way, God's way of living by love, and those who have transitioned into spirit now see that, and they want to share it with us. Their intention is to strengthen the love and connection they started with us while they were in body.

∾ CHAPTER 40 ∾

$\mathcal{M}$y testimony of believing we can talk with our loved ones in spirit started years ago when I was young and it was validated when Faye came into my life, or rather the validation came by her life.

I met Faye at school through a mutual friend when we were about thirteen. It was shortly after the transition of another loved one who was very close to me. It wasn't long before Faye and I were inseparable. It was the kind of connection that was rare and didn't come along very often. I always felt lucky that she picked me as a friend because she carried with her the energy of an angel. We shared much in common, including our love of animals, music, running, and the outdoors. I taught her how to play the guitar; she taught me about angels and the afterlife.

A couple of years after we met, she showed up one day with a furry friend she was babysitting. Lucky was his name. We got into a conversation about Lucky, and it evolved into her saying to me that if a white dog ever came to me, it was because it was sent to me by someone in spirit, by someone who loved me very much. What she said that day has always stuck with me and, yes, I wonder about who sent me Frizz.

The years brought us closer and even with our high school graduation the connection remained. Along came the day that Faye met and married what she thought to be the man of her dreams. We were both excited, being the typical twenty-year–olds— she newly married and me engaged. It was only a couple of weeks after her marriage things changed drastically.

The problems began, full force, and Faye started to see a side of her new husband she hadn't seen before. We kept in contact as much as we could, which had gotten more difficult as they had moved back to northern California. Our talks on the phone became far and few between, but the letters continued almost daily. Her letters told me the problems were much bigger than just an unhappy marriage. Faye and her husband had only been married a short time when she left him and came back to southern California with the intention of divorcing him. Her family and friends were very concerned as the situation was bad and we were all fearful of the outcome. She lived constantly in fear, which was hard to watch.

The day Faye and I met at the park, the same park that Frosty and I, many years later, would call home for our daily runs, Faye was scared and agitated. We sat together for a few hours and talked about how scary things were for her. She talked about the fear she had of how her life was going to end. As we talked, she became calmer, almost at peace. She expressed her desire to be at my wedding and to be my maid of honor, but by the end of our time together we were ready to admit that she wasn't going to be there. Admitting that to each other opened the door for us to express the love and the closeness we had always felt for each other and to talk openly about Faye's upcoming transition. She made it clear that we would talk again, when she was in spirit. We were both at peace with the things we had talked about.

When it was time to go, we said good-bye, not good-bye-I'll-see-you-tomorrow, but goodbye, I'll see you in spirit, knowing I would not see her again in body. There was no fear, and neither of us cried.

A couple of days after Faye and I met in the park, her transition became complete at the hands of her husband.

Faye and I had been friends in body for only eight years. She's been in spirit now for thirty years and we are closer than we ever were. She's always been there when I called her, walking beside me, guiding me when times were tough. She gave me many gifts while she was in body, but the biggest gifts have come with her in spirit.

Faye is the validation and strength behind my belief that our loved ones are still here, that we can communicate with them, and that they are helping us even while they're in spirit. She is my validation that love does conquer all, even the barriers of what some call death.

Communicating and connecting is possible because there is no death. Even today as I write, Faye sits in a tree just off to the right of me. She smiles with the calmness of an angel and the surety of one who knows, and I am grateful for her wisdom and her willingness to share that wisdom with me. Through her, I know our loved ones are still here and that they are continually talking with us. Has she been there twenty-four seven? Probably, however there are times when I talk with her that I don't feel or see her right away. It's just like when I call one of my friends in body who might be tied up doing something else, but they call me back as soon as they can. It's the same with Faye.

Those in spirit can be everywhere at once, so it never takes them long to connect with us, as long as we're open. With Faye, I feel there are times she has pushed me to trust that I don't need her as much as I think I do, and her words are, "You *can* do this."

I learned from Faye that it is me who has to ask for her, that she is always there and available the same way God is to all of us—but it has to be me opening up the phone lines.

She taught me to believe in the signs that she sent me. It was Faye who was there with me, showing me. She taught me that I had to keep asking and keep believing. Like becoming a better piano player, I had to practice to get good at it.

I learned that people in spirit love the acknowledgment as much as those of us in body. I found that when I acknowledged Faye, Frosty, and anyone else I talked with in spirit, it was easier to connect with them the next time. Whether in spirit or in body, we all love those way-to-go moments!

It was Faye who taught me to be grateful for the signs before, during, and after they came. Being grateful brought more connection in all ways. Am I grateful now, thirty years later that Faye transitioned so early in life? I don't know, but what I do know is that if I focus on what I have instead of what I don't have, life is full of more love, joy, happiness, and life!

A Letter From Frosty

My name is Frosty. I am a golden retriever. I came here to do a job for God. I am the same as everyone else, but I came in a body that is covered in fur. God chose me because I could teach best what Mama needed to learn. I am a teacher, a guide, a companion, and a director. I direct so the highest good can be done for all. I love my family as much as you do. I stay with them because I love them. I stay with them because it's my heart's desire to help them and because it helps me and it helps you.

My mama learns best when the lessons come from me, so I volunteered, well, *jumped* at the chance to be her guide. We all have teachers who love us and want the best for us. I am her teacher and she is mine.

I love being here with my family, being here now in this way, because I am still teaching, still learning, and still loving, but I'm freer now and I can move around a lot faster. I can be everywhere at once, with everyone all the time, I feel such happiness, joy, and love! I work daily to show and teach my mama that same way of life that I have now. I see that happiness can be attained in and out of a body. I see that our ultimate lesson is love, but I knew that before I put on the furry body suit because God told me just like he tells everyone.

I listened because I wanted my mama to know love, so I learned as fast as I could so I would know what to do when the time came to teach her. I was quiet and I listened hard and I paid close attention when God whispered in my ear. I learned about love and tried not to tear up the house or chew up any toys, but sometimes I couldn't help it. That was my way of teaching Mama to slow down and stop and get back to love. Sometimes I brought sticks into the house, but I always practiced unconditional love and forgiveness and I taught Mama what I learned.

I prayed with her at night and I prayed with her each morning. I brought God into her life and into her heart. I brought her joy so she could sing. When I had gotten really good at my job and had taught Mama all that I could in my furry body suit, God released me from it and now I can teach Mama even more about a love that goes even deeper than before.

My heart wants to burst at how big the love is now and how far it spreads out into my mama's heart. My heart lives with her heart, and together we can teach more love.

My name is Frosty, and I am a spirit of love—a love that goes on forever and ever. I am the same, and it is the same for you as for me. The people you love are still with you. They are with you, helping you, guiding you, and loving you always.

Are you always loving them…?

My name is Bethany-Elizabeth. I have a golden retriever named Frosty: then, now, and forever.

GRATITUDE TO:

All of you who have helped make Frosty's book a success.

And to

Cam – for being Frosty's biggest play toy from beginning to end!

Debi – my coach, my friend and my soul sister. Thanks for believing in me and in Frosty. And Goldie – for encouraging Frosty to shine, and for reminding me to always look on the bright side.

Dr. Cohn – for all the Scooby snacks and the sincere love with which you gave them to Frizz; and Dr. Christine – for the love you gave me.

Setrak – for the hours you worked to make Frosty look as strong and healthy as he is. www.sublimefotosbrea.com

Dwayne – for giving Frosty and me an extra six months. You truly are a reiki master; and Shelley – for holding my hand through one of the darkest times in my life. You were my flashlight in the dark.

Frank – for the countless trips to the feed store, grocery store, and deli, and for supporting this book, with blind trust without ever knowing what it was about. Frosty and Princess, thank you.

Heidi – for hand-making Frosty's favorite place to lay and for giving me the daughter I never had; and Brandon – how can words compare to the support, time, enthusiasm, and love with which you jumped into this project? I could not have done it without you.

Paul – for keeping the car cool, the chicken hot, buying the biggest toys and for taking good care of me when Mama couldn't.

Artemisa – for overcoming very challenging obstacles to keep the heart of Frosty connected to my soul and for loving him so very much. He is forever sending you bluebirds.

Brayden, Jaden and Jami – for showing me that you can see Frosty, and for helping me to hear him say "I'm still here". Christ said "and so the children shall lead", and lead us they have.

Melissa – I don't think there are words that express what I feel. You have helped to make this journey not only possible, but you have helped to fill it with love. Your passion for animals and your intuitive abilities were a miracle throughout this process. It's no wonder Frosty hangs with you so much. Thanks for walking a very tough road with me and Frizz. I am forever grateful.

Leslie – gosh… You've been by my side for so much and for so long. Your big heart shined through even a storm I thought I couldn't survive, and I wouldn't have if it weren't for you. I know God sent you. Thanks for sharing your dad with me and for becoming my mom when I needed it most. You loving Frosty the way that you do is the reason you can still see him and the reason he is still here for us both. Thanks for always wearing your heart on your sleeve. I love you.

Karyn – you are the greatest mom Emily could have. We are together and we are guiding the process of this book. Thanks for helping my mama. She loves you and so do I.

Liza and Little Bit – as always, I remember, and I love you both. Thanks for showing me that you're still here.

Tim – for bringing Frosty home. I could say more Tim, but I'm hoping you get the fullness of what I am unable to say.

Eddie – for lifting Frosty to the angels. Bam Bam, Frosty, and Angelie, are forever grateful for the love and the gift you have with our furry friends. They love you and so do I and yes, you're right, they are still with you, always on your back. It's their gift to you.

Faye – for teaching me that God speaks to us through animals, and for sticking by my side and being there for Frizz when he needed you most. You truly are one of my angels.

And to God and my universal support team. There are too many to list all of you by name, but I thank you all for guiding me, loving me, and sending me Frizz. To me, and for me, he truly is a master teacher and only all of you would know that.

Frosty – my teacher, my guide and my friend, for choosing me and for so very much more that you will have to read through my heart to hear. I love you, sweet precious, and I would still love to know, "How do you hug a spirit"?

13639550R00175

Made in the USA
Lexington, KY
11 February 2012